MW00531764

STORIES OF
HEAVEN
—— AND THE ——
AFTERLIFE

STORIES OF
HEAVEN
— AND THE —
AFTERLIFE

FIRSTHAND ACCOUNTS OF
REAL NEAR-DEATH EXPERIENCES

RANDY KAY &
SHAUN TABATT

© Copyright 2022—Randy Kay and Shaun Tabatt

All rights reserved. This book is protected by the copyright laws of the United States of America. This book may not be copied or reprinted for commercial gain or profit. The use of short quotations or occasional page copying for personal or group study is permitted and encouraged. Permission will be granted upon request. Unless otherwise identified, Scripture quotations are taken from the HOLY BIBLE, NEW INTERNATIONAL VERSION®, Copyright © 1973, 1978, 1984, 2011 International Bible Society. Used by permission of Zondervan. Please note that Destiny Image's publishing style capitalizes certain pronouns that refer to the Father, Son, and Holy Spirit, and may differ from some publishers' styles. Take note that the name satan and related names are not capitalized. We choose not to acknowledge him, even to the point of violating grammatical rules.

DESTINY IMAGE® PUBLISHERS, INC.
P.O. Box 310
Shippensburg, PA 17257-0310
"Promoting Inspired Lives."

This book and all other Destiny Image and Destiny Image Fiction books are available at Christian bookstores and distributors worldwide.

For more information on foreign distributors, call 717-532-3040.
Reach us on the Internet: www.destinyimage.com.

ISBN 13 TP: 978-0-7684-7181-6
ISBN 13 eBook: 978-0-7684-57182-3

For Worldwide Distribution.
1 2 3 4 5 6 7 8 / 26 25 24 23 22

TABLE OF CONTENTS

PREFACE

During the past twelve months Randy Kay and I have been on a mission to have honest conversations with people who have had real near-death experiences. This has led to numerous podcast episodes, several television interviews, multiple new book projects, and the first ever Christian afterlife virtual conference.

When we began this journey, we did not fully grasp what God had waiting down the road for us, but Randy and I are ever so thankful that we responded to God's prompting to begin helping more people share their afterlife stories. Looking at current trends and stories in Christian and mainstream media, I encounter content related to NDEs and the afterlife on an almost daily basis. God was clearly intentional in putting Randy and me out in front of a growing wave of interest that spans multiple segments of culture.

We continue to be blown away by the responses we receive to our content every single day. People who recently lost a loved one reach out and tell us that our conversations have given them hope and assurance that their loved one is in Heaven. Sick people report being healed. People who are depressed and suicidal report that they now have hope and peace. People who did not know Jesus report accepting Him as their Lord and Savior. It is amazing what God can do through an interview!

Following on the success of our previous book, *Real Near Death Experience Stories*, this new book shares four more impactful interviews from our podcast. Our prayer is that as you encounter the amazing testimonies in these pages, you will have the same sorts of God encounters reported by the people who watched and listened to these interviews. May Heaven become as real and tangible to you as it is to the people whose stories you encounter in this book.

Shaun Tabatt
Laurens, South Carolina, June 2022

CHAPTER 1

WHAT ARE WE TO MAKE OF ALL OF THESE NEAR-DEATH EXPERIENCES?

A near-death experience (NDE) is when a person is close to death or has clinically died after the heart stops and, after recovering, reports an otherworldly account, oftentimes an out-of-body experience where they can see their body as a third party, or some sort of vision of Heaven or hell. This can be described as a transphysical experience where the person is conscious of their self and capable of seeing and hearing—without the full functioning of the heart or brain. The person retains memory of the out-of-body event and appears to have vivid recall of the experience absent normal neurological functions.

Furthermore, the transphysical self is aware of itself, its surroundings, and its uniqueness from others in a way that is more than simply self-consciousness. The supernatural body is like an ethereal remnant of the physical body and is not limited by any physical restrictions like gravity or solid objects. These experiences can completely transform the individual as they enter another realm and oftentimes experience life reviews, encounter deceased loved ones or divine entities, feel a sense of well-being, and eventually return to life having been forever changed.

Transformation through Jesus Christ lies at the core of Christianity, and Christians who experience an NDE describe an overwhelming love while encountering Jesus. Just as the gospel of Christ causes transformation, so too transformation for the NDE survivor can result from a believer's encounter with Christ within a new body. Upon resuscitation from near-death, the survivor often recounts a vision of Heaven or some other ethereal environment.

There are no statements against near-death experiences in the Bible, but there is a description of the apostle Paul being caught up to the third Heaven in 2 Corinthians 12:2-4, possibly following his stoning in Lystra. It is generally believed in Christianity that any real encounter with Jesus in Heaven will align with God's Word (the Bible) and bring Jesus Christ glory.

One Scripture that speaks to the transphysical body described in the NDE is,

So will it be with the resurrection of the dead. The body that is sown is perishable, it is raised imperishable; it is sown in dishonor, it is raised in glory; it is sown in weakness, it is raised in power; it is sown a natural body, it is raised a spiritual body. If there is a natural body, there is also a spiritual body (1 Corinthians 15:42-44).

Another common description is the light experienced by NDEers: *"And there will be no more night; they need no light of lamp or sun, for the Lord God will be their light, and they will reign forever and ever"* (Revelation 22:5). The almost universal feeling of joy told by Christian NDEers is described, *"He will wipe every tear from their eyes. There will be no more death or mourning or crying or pain, for the old order of things has passed away"* (Revelation 21:4).

Over 60 Bible verses reference near-death or close-to-death experiences. There are several similarities between the Christian view of Heaven and near-death experiences. Christian theologists like John Burke, who studied over 1,000 cases for 35 years, and Lee Strobel, who discovered over 900 scientific and medical journals relating to these experiences, determined that NDEs are consistent with Christian theology.

A preponderance of evidence in favor of NDEs as real and not induced by any hallucinogenic factors now point to these experiences as a valid indicator of life after physical life in this world.

A QUICK NOTE FROM SHAUN

One last thing we want to equip you with as we begin our journey into these amazing afterlife encounters is a list of things to be on the lookout for. As you become more familiar with near-death experiences, you will begin to see some common occurrences that show up in most of these accounts. We have found that being familiar with these common stages in most NDEs up front helps the reader to be better prepared to process and make sense of what our friends are sharing in their stories.

Here are the ten things to watch for:

1. *Out-of-body experience (OBE):* The experience of your spirit rising out of your body. You are often aware of the details of what is going on around your body, even though you are not in a conscious state.

2. *Tunnel:* As a person's spirit is transitioning from the physical world to the spiritual world, people often recount seeing and being pulled into a tunnel.

3. *Bright light:* There are many occurrences of bright lights during NDEs. They tend to be an indicator of coming into the proximity of God the Father, Jesus, and sometimes angels.

4. *Torment:* Many people recount torment by demons and/or an awful experience in hell before transitioning into Heaven.

5. *Cry for help:* Many people recount crying out for help during the above-mentioned time of torment. This often results in either Jesus or angels showing up to rescue them and escort them into Heaven.

6. *Life review:* A review of the good and bad things that you did in life. Many near-death experiencers tell us they were able to experience and feel how their actions impacted others from the other person's point of view.

7. *Encountering friends or loved ones:* People often report encountering deceased friends and family members in Heaven.

8. *Encountering animals/pets:* People often report encountering a beloved deceased pet in Heaven.

9. *Saturated in love:* Love permeates everything in Heaven. Many people say they felt completely and totally immersed in love during their time in Heaven.

10. *Communicating in Heaven:* You do not need to talk in Heaven. Communication is instantaneous. The best way we have come up with to describe it is spirit to spirit or thought to thought.

Now that you have an overall context for what you are going to encounter in these testimonies, let's begin the journey. Our prayer is that each conversation will stretch you, encourage you, and bring you closer to a full and complete realization that the resurrected Jesus is real and Heaven is a real place He longs for you to call home someday.

CHAPTER 2

MAN STUNG BY FIVE JELLYFISH DIES, ENCOUNTERS JESUS IN HEAVEN, AND IS FULLY HEALED WHEN HE WAKES UP

MEET IAN McCORMACK

New Zealand native Ian McCormack was in his late twenties and living a carefree surfing lifestyle in some of the most beautiful places on the planet. One fateful night in 1982 he was night diving for lobster off the island of Mauritius when he was stung by five box jellyfish, one of the most venomous creatures in the world. A sting from a single box jellyfish can kill a person in under five minutes. Getting stung by five should have been beyond lethal.

In this conversation, Randy and Shaun go deep into Ian's Heaven experience, talking about what he heard and saw in Heaven, recounting his dramatic healing after he woke up in the morgue, and unpacking the many surprising experiences that transpired after Ian left the hospital.

INTERVIEW WITH IAN McCORMACK

RANDY: One sting from a jellyfish can kill a human being in a matter of minutes and Ian was stung by five box jellyfish! This fascinating story is simply going to blow your mind.

Ian, thanks for joining us from New Zealand. We are eager to get right into your story.

IAN: Randy and Shaun, it is great to be with you guys. It was the Word of God that touched my heart and the love of God that changed me through this experience. I can testify that I am here today because of a praying mum. Even though I was a million miles away from God, it was my mum's prayers that changed me forever.

I grew up in New Zealand, which is like Heaven on Earth. I loved the outdoors so much that my mother thought I had fish blood in me. Most of my free time was spent surfing, diving, and swimming. As a young man, I was just fascinated by the ocean. I am quite sure I watched every Jacques Cousteau program on TV. I was captivated by it and desired to be a marine biologist. When I found out marine biology required a seven-year degree, I decided to pursue a degree in veterinary science at Lincoln University in New Zealand.

While I was working for the New Zealand Dairy Board, my best friend, Tony McCartney, a good Irish mate, said to me, "Would you like to travel the world surfing?" We had just finished watching a movie called *Endless Summer*. It had captivated us. No winter, no wet suits, just get our surfboards and travel the tropics. And so I said, "Yes, I'm in." We grabbed our boards and began to travel through Australia, Indonesia, Sri Lanka, South Africa, and Mauritius Reunion. We spent two years surfing the world, and in April 1982 I ended up back in Mauritius, living with a local Creole fisherman. You know the Rastafarians, the Peter Tosh guys. They said, "Do not worry, mon, be happy, smoke, more hashish."

They were laid-back, phenomenal athletes and awesome friends. They taught me to night dive. I had dived in many different parts of the world, but at night that was a whole new experience. When we went out diving, we would see parafish sound asleep on the reef and beautiful crabs and lobster out walking on the reef. It dropped off 12-14,000 feet where we dove along the edge of the lagoon.

On April 19, 1982, I dropped into the ocean and could vaguely make out what I thought was a transparent cuddle fish because I had never seen a jellyfish that looked like this. It was bell-shaped with two finger-like tentacles. Had I known what it was, I would have immediately gotten out of the water, but unfortunately, I had never seen a photograph of a box jellyfish. So right in front of me was potentially the deadliest creature known to man. The neurotoxin from a box jellyfish is 100 times more lethal than a cobra!

I saw it, took note of it, but continued to dive. I found the water in the tropics quite warm, so I was wearing a wetsuit with a short-sleeved vest. This meant my forearms, neck, and ankles were all exposed. The Creole divers who had lived there all their lives in the tropics had put on full wet suits with rubber hoods and booties, leaving them all encased in a layer of protective rubber. My exposed skin was going to lead to a life-threatening issue this fateful night.

Suddenly something smashed into my arm and it felt like I had been shocked by a volt of electricity, like someone touching my arm with a branding iron under the water. Shaken by it, I could not see what hit me. Then another one hit me. This time I saw it was a jellyfish. That was when I realized I was in a soup of thousands of jellyfish that had been washed up onto the reef. Before I could get to the reef and climb up to talk to the divers, I was hit four times across my forearm. My arm was blistered as though I had been whipped across my arm. My skin was raised and looked like it was about to burst.

As I sat there dazed and staring at my arm, my friend Simone, the Creole fisherman, said, "How come you not know?" I said, "I have not known this one." He said, "Go quickly to the hospital" The trouble is, we were at least half an hour away from the hospital and were standing on an outer reef. They lowered me into the water and dragged me to the fishing boat. And as my right arm, which was partly paralyzed, was dragged up into the boat, I got hit a fifth time. I thought, *What on earth have I done to deserve this?* That is when I had a flood of memories of the things that I had done wrong in my life.

I thought, *Well, I forgot about that. Gosh, I did that too.* How many of us have short memories? Been there and done that. Well, at this stage in my life, I no longer believed in any form of God. I was an atheist. I thought that was something that my mother did and my grandmother, who was in the choir. This is for old ladies, people who need religion. For me, my scientific background at university had knocked any form of faith or belief in God out. So here I am confronted with my mortality and confronted with the fact that I could potentially die.

When you see black men turn white, it is quite unnerving. And these guys loved me. I was as close as a brother to them. When I saw them panicking, I knew that I was in serious trouble. They told me to urinate on my arm to nullify the neurotoxin. That is one way to release the tentacles that were microscopically embedded into my skin. Next, I began to apply a manual tourniquet because I had no rope. I peeled my wetsuit off because I could hardly breathe. I got changed into my sweats and a T-shirt and a young boy began taking me toward the shore. I said to Simone and the other divers, "Come with me, please." Simone said, "Ian, there is no motor. Let the boy take. He has only got a pole. He must get you to the hospital quickly." It was a fatal mistake. They should have come with me.

When we got to the beach, I stood up and tried to walk but collapsed. To my horror, the neurotoxin had paralyzed the right-hand side of my body within that brief period of time. I fell headlong into the bottom of the boat, trying to brace myself on my fallen arm. The kid motioned for me to put my arm around his neck and he dragged me bodily. I do not know how he did it, but he got me up the sandy coral beach to the main road. It was 11 p.m. when we got up there, so there was not anyone around. The boy started to freak out. He could see that I was dying. He knew his brothers were still out there on the reef, so he wanted to go out and rescue them. In my limited French, I was trying to get him to call a doctor, an ambulance, a police officer, or anybody who could help. But of course, this was 1982. You could not just pull out your cell phone and make a call.

I was feeling overwhelmed, weak, and tired. I laid down on the side of the road and my eyes just automatically began to shut.

Suddenly, I heard a man's voice saying, "Son, if you close your eyes, you will never wake again." It was so clear and so audible that it caused me to turn to look in the direction of the man's voice. Amazingly, there was no one there. I thought, *Where is he calling from and how on earth did I hear that?* And then I realized that no one was there. I had just heard an invisible man speak audibly to me.

I found out later that Jesus said, "My sheep hear My voice." Well, I was a black sheep, a million miles away from God, but what is amazing is that Jesus said, "I go looking for the lost sheep." He goes searching for them. And of course, at that time I did not realize I was lost. I thought I understood life. I was fairly together. I had no concept that there was a living God that could speak to mankind. So I ran the thought through: *close your eyes and you will never wake again.* And of course, I knew from my own physiology training as a lifeguard and from veterinary science that you cannot go to sleep with a neurotoxin. That is not sleep; it is a coma, which would lead to certain death. I believe, had I not heard His voice, which I now know to be the voice of God, I would have died on the beach.

Hearing God's voice was a turning point. I stood up, summoned whatever adrenaline I had left in me, and began looking for help. As I stood up, I was amazed I had not seen them before. A hundred meters down the road were three Indian taxi drivers at a small petrol station. I slowly staggered toward them. They saw me coming and thought I was drunk. As I got up to them, I said, "Look, I am not drunk. I have been stung by five box jellyfish. This is deadly. I need antiserum. I must get to the hospital. Can you help me?" They said, "We can, but how much money will you pay?"

I said, "Fifty dollars? One hundred dollars? Who cares, man?" And they said, "Let me see your money, white man, and we take you." Well, of course I did not have $100 on me; I had been diving. So I just mumbled out the words "I do not have the money with me." When they heard that, all three just walked away, and I realized that in this part of the world, with no money, you could die. I was near South Africa, so there was a lot of animosity and racial hatred, which I was now on the receiving end of. Then I heard that voice again asking me, "Son, are you willing to beg for your life?"

I thought, *Beg for my life?* That is a brilliant idea. I had not thought of it. And I turned to see where the man was. So, for a second time, I have this man speaking to me. He said, "Will, you beg for your life?" I thought, *Well, I am sure these men have never seen a white man beg for anything in Mauritius.* So I quickly fell to my knees, grabbed my paralyzed right hand, bowed my head, looked down at their feet, and begged for my life as an act of humility.

Two of them continued walking away, and I thought that was a bad sign, but the third young man walked over without saying a word and helped me into his taxi. I thanked him profusely. I said, "Man, that's so good. Thank you." As we raced toward the hospital, he then began to ask me how he was going to get the $100 that I had promised him. He said, "What's your hotel room? Where do you stay?" I said, "Well, I live with a Creole fisherman. I do not stay in a hotel." He said, "You lied to me." And he suddenly changed from a demeanor of helpfulness to anger. I said, "Well, I live with the fisherman in Tamaran Bay." He said, "Oh, you stay in the hotel there, the Chinese hotel." I said, "No, no." He said, "You not pay me. You lie to me. Why you lie to me?"

I said, "Look, I am not lying. I am a traveling surfer. I am not a tourist." But these words meant nothing to him. He said, "No money? I will take you to the nearest tourist hotel and they can look after you." So he pulled in front of the hotel and told me to get out. At this point, I realized when I tried to move that both legs were now completely paralyzed. The poison had now taken out both legs. I said, "Sir, I cannot walk. I have a large amount of money. If you get me to the hospital, you name your price." To my horror, he reached over, took my safety belt off, opened the door, and before I knew what had happened, pushed me straight out of his taxi. As I fell to the ground, he drove off into the night and left me for dead.

At this point, I thought, *Well, why would you want to live on a planet like this? If your number is up, do yourself a favor and die here. It is pointless if this is how humanity treats a fellow man.* So I laid there, dying and giving up. It is funny how things come to mind. Suddenly, I had a recollection of my grandfather, who had fought through Gallipoli during the First World War against the Ottoman Turks and in the Second World War against Rommel. So, somehow I was recollecting a grandfather who was a military warrant officer, a professional soldier. I thought, *Here you are his grandson and you're giving up after being stung by five stupid jellyfish. You might as well die fighting, man. What is the point?*

I had seen men in battle. Most of my family was either involved in the military or farming. And I thought, *Why not just try?* So I grabbed clumps of grass in amongst the asphalt of the broken car park and began to pull myself bodily along the ground. I was getting very little movement, but at least I was trying. Then I looked up and someone was shining a flashlight at me. As I looked up, I could see one of the security guards. It was my drinking buddy Daniel. He was standing over me, saying, "What happened to you? I have never seen you like this. What are you doing in the car park, man? You have never crawled around the car park legless on a Friday night." So here I am crawling on the ground and he is thinking I am drunk or stoned or something.

Then he noticed the marks from the jellyfish, and as a fellow night diver and a fisherman, he instantly recognized them. So he reinforced the same thing the other divers had said: "It will kill you. The end." He scooped me up in his arms and raced into the Hotel Browns. The Chinese family that owned it was playing Mahjong by the swimming pool, drinking their black label, Johnny Walker. I was in the surreal position of being carried, and it is weird, man, time just seemed to unfold in slow motion. Next, I was lowered into a chair near the three Chinese owners and thought, *Daniel, tell them. You are a flipping local. You speak French Creole.* But of course I realized that as a Creole, he couldn't speak unless spoken to.

One of the men said, "You drunk?" I said, "No, no, my arm. I have been hit by five box jellyfish. Deadly. I must get to the hospital. Can you help me?" One of the owners looked over and he could see the marks on my arm. And he went, "Oh, you stupid white boy. Why did you put the needle in your arm? The old men take opium with a pipe. Why did you put the needle in your arm?" He immediately thought that the marks were from heroin, that I had been chasing the dragon, that I must be mainlining smack or something, shooting up. Unfortunately, in those years I was trying to look like the Beatles. Remember Woodstock? My hair was down here, man. And so he must have thought I was just a druggie, you know? And I said, "Look, this is not drugs. This is from a jellyfish."

They ignored me and resumed playing their game, thinking I was just some drunk tourist.

And then as I was sitting there, I saw out of the corner of my eye that my right hand and arm were beginning to spasm. Then my jaw began to spasm. Next, my right hand began to shake violently and I go into what I can only describe as the death rattle. I had seen someone with epilepsy have a grand mal seizure. It was similar in its bodily shaking, but this was not epilepsy. This was a neurotoxin causing my body to violently react to the poison within my system. As I was shaking to bits, the three men physically tried to restrain me, but I was throwing them off. As quickly as it started, it stopped. And I went ice cold. I could feel a cold encroaching death coming into my body, starting in the bone marrow of my feet and moving up like necrosis into the core of my body.

I began to shiver and said, "Please, give me blankets, please help me." Three men ran out of the room. The next minute, two of them were back, wrapping me up in blankets. The third one for some reason was holding a glass of milk. He tried to pour it down my throat and I realized that he was thinking I had ingested a toxin, so the milk might nullify it. So at least he was thinking. I said, "Sir, I do not need the milk. I need someone who can take me. I can see your car in the car park. Please take me in your Mercedes to the hospital now, or I will die in front of you." I expected it to be a mere formality. Unfortunately, the man looked at his car, put his hand on my shoulder, and said, "My car, no we cannot take my car. You must wait for an ambulance. Do not worry, white man."

Have you ever wanted to hit someone? He was so close. I thought, *How dare you not take me in your car? What kind of sick human being are you?* So I tried to hit him, but my right hand would not move because it was paralyzed. So I tried my left. I thought that if there was a small amount of strength, I could grab his shirt, work him into my forehead, and teach him a lesson in humanity about what not to do with a dying man. I wanted to flipping rearrange his face. So I was about to whack this guy when I heard the voice for the third time. He said, "Son, if you hit this man, the neurotoxin is so close to your heart, the adrenaline rush will kill you."

It stopped me. I was so close to hitting him and there was this voice again. It's true: if I had hit him, it would have hastened my death. I thought, *Well, I can control my anger, look away, and get him later.* So I thought, *Yeah, plan B.* So I turned to my right just to control the anger and suppress it, and to my amazement an ambulance pulled into the car park. Suddenly Daniel appeared from nowhere with another security guard. They scooped me up out of the chair and raced toward the entrance of the hotel to get me into the ambulance. I realized, *Oh my goodness, I was about to kill myself, and here comes an ambulance.* Interestingly, God often leaves things to the last second. I do not know why He does that, but you can manifest and kick off when He is about to rescue you.

As I was lying in the back of the ambulance, the Frenchman who was driving did not say anything; he just drove. I was shivering, shaking, freezing, and dying. As we began climbing the ridge toward the hospital, my legs began to elevate, which was the worst thing that could have happened. The neurotoxin in my lymphatic system and my blood was beginning to drain into my lungs and my heart. I could feel death enveloping me, shutting down what was left of my bodily functions. As this was happening, I could feel my mind shutting down from the poison.

I started thinking that this was simply crazy. After all this, I might not even make it to the hospital. The next minute, it was like a video clip began to play and I could see a child with snowy white hair, a teenager. Suddenly I realized I was seeing my life race in front of my eyes in a matter of seconds. I knew it was me. I had heard of this phenomenon happening just before a person dies. I then thought, *Well, perhaps I am nearly dead.* So I did a quick physiological check of my vital signs. My mind succinctly said, *Yes, son, you are nearly dead. You may not make it.* I thought, *Well, if I die and do not make it to the hospital, is there life after death, or is there nothing?* I thought, *Well, atheist/evolutionist, when you die, nothing happens. Ash, dust, and worms get you. Cessation of life.*

It's finished, right? I thought, but I am a gambling atheist. The gamblers go, "You have been wrong before, son. You know?" And I thought, *Well, as a gambler I have heard many opinions: Buddhism, Taoism, Darwinism, Confucianism, Catholicism, and humanism. Man, there are a ton of isms out there.* So I laid there and thought, *Well, there are many isms; which one is true?* I thought, *I have no clue. I will find out soon.* It was a bit like playing Russian roulette: I would find out which one was true shortly. I was not afraid to die. I would soon find out. As all this was racing in front of me, suddenly, miraculously, I saw my mum on her knees, praying. This just shook me to the core. I had no idea until I talked to my mum later, on the other side of the world, that my mother had just seen my face, seen that I was nearly dead, and God had audibly spoken. It was only the second time she had ever heard the audible voice of God, and He had said, "Your elder son, Ian, is nearly dead. Pray for him now."

And my mum ran into the bedroom where she prays and fell on her knees and began pleading with God to save her son and to save his soul. And my father had no idea what was going on. He was like, "What's wrong, honey? What's wrong?" She told him, "Ian's about to die." Dad told me later what mum was doing. It appears mothers know when their children are in trouble. They have another sense; they can be a million miles away from their kids but they know when something is going wrong. Those mothers, thank God, can pray and know what is happening. And here I was seeing my mum. She was the only Christian in the family, the only real believer on her knees praying. She then pleaded with me. She said, "Son, no matter what you have done wrong, no matter how far from God you may be, no matter how bad, call out to God from your heart. He will hear you, son. He will forgive you. He will forgive you, Ian. Call out to God."

It was so emotive. It was so powerful, as though Mum was in the ambulance with me, reaching out and touching something that was inside me that had not been touched since I was a small child when I used to kneel by my bed with her each night and pray the Lord's Prayer. And I was lying there, going, "Mum, I do not believe in God. It is too late. I have committed too many sins. I'd be a hypocrite praying." My mum just kept saying, "No, son. Pray. He will forgive you. He will forgive you now." And I was going, "Well, which God, Mum? Everyone thinks that their God's the right one. Who do I pray to?" And Mum did not say a thing, but I knew she was a Christian. So I said, "God, if You are real, show Yourself to me. I need to see to believe. Show me Yourself and I will pray right now."

No one appeared except Mum. And I thought, *Well, Mum is a true believer. She prays only to Jesus. Could Mum be right?* Well, how many hate it when your mother's right? But anyhow, I later thought, *Well, Mum, this is the time to be right.* And I thought, *Well, what would I pray that is Christian?* I thought about when I was a little boy and Mum prayed the Lord's Prayer. Christian Jesus. Got it. So I tried to pray it and my mind went completely blank. I had never prayed this prayer before in my life. And Mum said, "Ian, do not pray from your mind. Pray from your heart." "But, Mum, my heart's like stone. I am so cynical." I thought, *I am so unbelieving that, God, if You exist, if You are out there, if You see anything good in my heart, help me to pray the Lord's Prayer. I can't remember it.* Instantly words appeared in front of me: Forgive us our trespasses and sins. I thought, *Well, these are powerful words, but how can God almighty, should He exist, forgive me by my saying just these words?* I thought, *Well, I do not have time to list my sins and I cannot even remember them all.*

So I said, "God, if You are there, I am sincerely asking You to forgive me of all my sins. I have certainly broken many of Your commandments. Please forgive me. If it's at all possible, forgive me." The words just seemed to disappear. Suddenly more words came up in front of me: Forgive those who have trespassed and sinned against you. I could do that by nature of being taught, not to be vengeful or vindictive. I could forgive anyone I was sure had harmed me in my life. "God, I forgive anyone who has sinned against me." As I said it, the Indian taxi driver's face appeared a foot away, and the voice said, "Will you forgive this man for pushing you out of his taxi tonight and leaving you for dead in front of the hotel?" I thought, *You must be joking. Why the heck should I forgive him?* Suddenly the Chinese hotel owner appeared, and the voice said, "Will you forgive this man for not taking you in his car to the hospital and for leaving you to die in the hotel?"

I had other plans for their lives, all right. I was going to lay my hands upon them, but it was not like a priest. My hands were going to be around their flipping throats. I laid there realizing this was the fourth time I had heard this man's voice, but this man was attaching Himself now directly to a prayer my mother said was taught by the Son of God, by almighty God. Sometimes men are a bit thick. It takes a while to join the dogs, you know? They are also very arrogant and proud. I laid there and thought, *Oh my goodness! That could be almighty God who is asking me to forgive real people, not just mumble off some prayer*—which I had done as a child to keep my mum happy, meaningless repetition—*I must forgive real people who have harmed me.*

And these men would truly be the tip of an iceberg. I said, "Lord, if You can forgive me, I will forgive these men. It would be an absolute miracle if You could wash all my sins away and give me a fresh start. I will then forgive these men. Never touch them. Never seek them out. Never harm them all the days of my life." As I said that, their faces instantly disappeared. Fresh words: Thy will be done on Earth as it is in Heaven. What the heck did that mean? I'd prayed it millions of times. What was, thy will, God's will be done? I thought, *Well, so far, it's my will done. And it has nothing to do with Heaven. And it's a complete train wreck here on Earth.* I said, "God, I have never surrendered the will of my life, the leadership of my life over to the lordship of Christ. I do not even know what You are doing in Heaven. I certainly have not lived anything that looks godly."

So I laid there and said, "God, if You help me through this, I will find Your will. I will try to accomplish Your will on Earth all the days of my life. I surrender my life to You." As I was praying this, I realized I was praying to Jesus, not only as Savior but also as Lord. Those who call upon the name of the Lord shall be saved. And Jesus had said, if you do not forgive others who have sinned against you their sins, God, the heavenly Father, will not forgive you your sins against Him. So your unforgiveness and bitterness and hatred will nullify your repentance and save a lot of counseling. So I was lying there. I was forgiving. Somehow meeting with God. I did not know what to do: cry, weep, laugh?

The whole prayer came. And for the first time on the planet at the age of 26, I got the Lord's Prayer, a personal revelation and encounter. I prayed from my heart, those words. And as I finished the Lord's Prayer, peace enveloped my spirit. It was as though the hand of God came in and sealed my heart with His peace and presence. And I knew that I was completely accepted, that somehow, I had made peace with my maker through this prayer. Jesus said that if you pray to the Father this prayer, you can make peace with Him. A peace that surpasses understanding, a peace that will never leave you. I did not know any of the theology that would have told me I was born again. All I knew was that I had called upon the name of the Lord and He had heard me.

SHAUN: Ian, give us a little context for how much time had taken place with what you have shared so far. As we talked about earlier, getting stung by one box jellyfish can kill the average person in just a few minutes, but you got stung by five. You journeyed a very windy path to get to the hotel and eventually the ambulance. What is the total timeframe from when you first got stung to when you arrived at the hospital?

IAN: It took us five minutes to get to shore. I should have died there. I heard God's voice and fought. I hobbled down the road another couple of minutes. It was another five minutes down the road to the hotel, another five minutes of sitting there shaking until the ambulance arrived. So we were 15 to 20 minutes into the experience and it was still a 10-minute ride to the hospital. So it was a half-hour from when I was first stung until then. So I was clinging to my life and I was cognitive that I was fighting this poison. I was using every ounce of energy. Most people slip into a coma and do not realize that they need to fight it. As I was coming through this experience of praying, everything went in slow motion. Years ago, I had been in a car roll where the vehicle had rolled, and I noticed that time slowed down. I talked to God about this later. He said, "Ian, I wish that none would perish. There is more grace given to men in those dying moments. I am eternal. I can slow time down." I have seen men in war who talked to Him, a bullet was coming for them, missing them. Guys in car wrecks, cars flipping, everything going into slow motion. People with heart attacks instantly know. They have opportunities to potentially pray and talk to God, even though it looks instantaneous.

RANDY: One thing that is so fascinating to me is, you had all of these people who were rejecting you in terms of not offering their help. And then you had several encounters with this voice that came to you. Who do you think that voice was? Do you think it was an angel? Was it the Lord speaking to you?

IAN: The Lord Himself, God Himself. It says in Isaiah that what separates us from hearing His voice is our sin. But when we start to come before Him, God speaks and talks to nonbelievers all the time. The question is, do we know who is speaking? Do we know His voice? Are we willing to turn from our sins? And so I was hearing this voice and realizing this was the Lord. This was

God Himself, because as I got further into the experience, I met Him in the heavenly realm. It was Him talking to me directly. So, at that point, I knew it was God but had not yet met Him.

RANDY: So this is God speaking to you and He is intervening and telling you what to do and what not to do. Meanwhile, these others are not helping, and by all intents and purposes, you should have been dead by this time.

IAN: I should have slipped into a coma and died within five minutes, ten minutes maximum. I talked to several doctors who deal with this kind of stuff and they said, "Even if we have injected a serum of antivenom or antitoxin, we are taught to continually slap the patient to keep them awake so they are fighting alongside us. Even though they have had the antiserum or antivenom given, they must stay conscious. The patient must be physically engaged in fighting against the poison. In my case, the antiserum would not have stopped it anyhow. This is a top neurotoxin, so it attacks your neurological system, systematically paralyzing you until it hits the vital organs of the heart and the brain. When it hits your brain, you are dead.

RANDY: Was this antitoxin administered to you in the ambulance or at the hospital?

IAN: No. When they got me into the hospital, they put me in a wheelchair because I was paralyzed. They raced me inside, but it can take a while to see a doctor in the middle of the night. The nurse put the blood pressure cuff onto my arm. The first time, there was no measurable pulse. She looked confused and tried another one. Still no pulse. I realized that this is what is called a crash mode. In other words, your extremities shut down under trauma. Under this kind of duress, the body goes into self-preservation. This nurse had never seen someone with their eyes still open but their extremities were shutting down and they had no measurable pulse.

The ambulance driver could see that the nurse had lost the plot. He had seen and dealt with more trauma than she had. He ripped the cuff off my arm, pushed the nurse to one side, and raced me directly through to the doctors, knowing that I was in crash mode. At this point, I was nearly gone.

The doctors were examining me when the nurse raced in with two blood pressure results, showing them that I had no pulse. Suddenly people started coming out of the woodwork. The old doctor did not even wait; he started filling a syringe with antiserum and injected it into me. More nurses arrived and began slapping my hand, trying to get a drip feed in for dehydration. The old doctor said, "Son, do not close your eyes, whatever you do. You need to fight this poison or you will die. We are trying to save your life."

RANDY: That's exactly what God had been telling you all along, now reiterated by the doctor.

IAN: One hundred percent. I was then watching my veins blow up like a bubble and nothing was moving. So they got three injections in and tried to manually massage it, and it was just rolling off their thumb and forefinger because my veins had collapsed. These poor doctors and nurses, they were trying their best, but I could see in their eyes that they were all freaking out. That's when the old doctor said, "Son, I am sorry. That is all we can do for you. You need to fight this poison and keep your eyes open. Do not close them."

They took me out of the wheelchair and laid me down on a recovery bed. That was the worst thing they could have done because it just spread the poison out. I could then feel the neurotoxin attacking. I could not speak or tilt my head. I could only barely close my eyelids. Each time I lifted them, they got worse. I thought, *I need to stop. I need to rest. I need to shut my eyes for a few minutes and try again. Time for a power nap.*

When I shut my eyes, it felt like the battle to stay alive had finished. As I was feeling this extraordinary release, I heard the flatline alarm go off on the heart monitor. My pulse was gone. Some people see a lot of stuff once they are dead, and of course, this was not just heart dead, because it was a neurotoxin. This was not a heart attack where you can be heart dead but not brain dead. I was killed by the poison. I was flatlined, everything, heart dead and brain dead. At the moment of death, I felt this extraordinary release and suddenly I was out of my body.

Many people talk about being able to look down and see people standing and talking during their out-of-body experience. Of course, what Jesus said is that when a man dies, his spirit leaves his body. You know, the physical body is just a clay vessel. It is ash to ash, dust to dust. Jesus said, "I am the resurrection of life. Those who believe in me, even though they die, yet they should live." So the physical body dies but the spirit of the man created in the image of God leaves. So, in a second, I was out of the hospital, in a completely different realm. But now I was awake, standing upright, and everything was pitch black.

I thought, *Did I just die? Have I just died and left my body or have I just woken up in the dark?* I was not sure how long I had been asleep. Well, I had to be alive, not dead. It was dark. Obviously my pupils were dilated and I had been asleep longer than I had thought. Sometimes you can go to sleep for a few seconds and it ends up that a few hours have passed. I thought, *Well, do not panic. Your pupils are dilated. Let them adjust to the dark. You will see some light.* So I then turned 360 degrees around looking for light. I began looking for a light switch, reaching out to my right, trying to not trip over anything. Of course, to my amazement, there was no wall. I went back to where my hospital bed should have been, looking for a lamp or a table.

Nothing. It was so dark I could not see my hand in front of my face; so I brought my hand toward where my face should have been and my hand passed straight through my head. That was impossible. I tried two hands. They both went straight through my face. Yet I could feel that I was there and my hands were there. When I tried to touch my body, I discovered there was no physical form. I was now in a realm where I was dead and out of my body. The only thing I could relate this to was Grandfather telling stories of people who had lost limbs in the war but who continued to experience what they call phantom pain. In my mind I was going, *Well, forget just losing an arm or a leg. You have potentially lost your entire human form that is back in that hospital, and you are potentially dead but also alive in a realm of complete darkness.*

That shook me. I then became very aware of a cold evil, an encroaching presence in the darkness. It was spiritual, not just physical. It felt like there was something in the darkness, aware of my presence, aware of my thoughts, now making a beeline for me. Then I heard men scream, "Shut up!" And I went, "I said nothing." They said, "You deserve to be here." Screaming my loudest I said, "Deserve to be where? Where am I now?" They said, "Man, you are in hell. Now shut up." I said, "I am good. I do not believe in hell. It is just a thing to terrify flipping weak-minded people. If this is hell, where is the party, where are the sex, drugs, and rock and roll?"

My understanding was that if you made it down to hell for some bizarre reason, everything you could not do on earth you could do down there. Well, it is ridiculously hard to grab a beer or hold a woman when you cannot touch anything. I was thinking, *Well, if this is hell, from a Christian point of view, shouldn't there be rotting corpses with maggots trying to eat them?* I thought, *Well, that can't happen because my maggoty body is back there in the hospital and this is a spiritual body.* I wondered where the demons and fire were. I was thinking about how there were all these beings around me trying to tune me in to the fact that I was in hell. I should have just shut my face since I deserved to be there just like they were. And then I was thinking, *Well, if there was fire down here, you would have light. You would see something.* I had no concept of that. Paul says in acts 26:18 that there are two kingdoms in the spirit realm, a kingdom of darkness ruled by satan and a kingdom of light ruled by almighty God. And I remembered something like Psalm 23 that you often hear read at funerals: *The Lord is my shepherd. I shall not want. Even though I walk through the valley of the shadow of death, I shall fear no evil.* What was amazing is that the evil was all around me but it could not touch me.

It was as though, and the Scriptures say it, greater is He within us than he who is in the world. Nothing can separate us from the love of God. Even though I walk through the valley of the shadow of death, surely goodness and mercy will follow me all the days of my life. So I was standing there recognizing that you cannot get hungry, you cannot do all the things you want to do, but God could potentially have judged me to this realm and held me in darkness. The Bible says *until the day of judgment*, so I thought then maybe that is when they get thrown into the fire. I did not know. I had never read the Bible, but that is exactly what the Bible says. At the final judgment, they will be cast into a lake of fire and brimstone. There will be a final judgment, but men are held there until then.

So I am standing there and pure light pierces through the darkness above me. It pinpoints me. It somehow had just singled me out amid that darkness. As it enveloped me, my entire body had a weightless sensation. I began to lift into this incredible light and I was moving up toward it. The source of this radiance was far above me as this was taking place. When I looked back, I could see the darkness was now far beneath me. I thought, *Man, is that wise to do?* And then I had a childhood, a Sunday school, memory of Lot's wife. The angel said, "We are going to deliver you out of Sodom and Gomorrah, but just a warning: we are about to destroy it. Whatever you do, do not look back." And of course, Lot's poor wife did the worst thing. She looked back and instantly turned into a pillar of salt.

Sometimes those Sunday school stories do stick. I started thinking, *No, do not look back. You do not want to go back into the darkness. Fix your eyes upon this radiance. At least you are going in the right direction.* As I kept moving up, I saw that I was being drawn into a circular-shaped opening. As I entered it, I became acutely aware. It was the beginning of a long narrow tunnel. As I looked along the length of it, I could see the source of the radiance at the farthest point. I realized that the tunnel was not the source of the light; it was only conducting pure light through it. And somehow it pulled me out of the darkness. Those walking in darkness have seen a great light, light shines in the darkness, and the darkness flees. I was now moving toward this light that was coming at me.

I watched the thick intense light hit me like a wave of radiance and my entire body was full of comfort. It was like a living emotion had just been given off from this light. But that was it: it was a living light. Another wave of light came up, bringing pure peace from the tip of my head to the base of my feet. And Jesus said, "Peace I give you. Not of this world." I then thought, *Well, in the light I might be able to see what I look like in the darkness.* My hand went straight through my face. So I turned my head to the right and my arm, hand, and fingers were transparent, full of white radiance. It was my hand. It responded and I could see it. And I remember reading later that we are transformed. Mortality takes on immortality. First the natural, then the heavenly. First the earthly, then the spiritual, but we shall be changed.

Flesh and blood will not inherit the kingdom of God, for God, who is the Father of lights, will bring us home and we will become sons and daughters of light. I was now seeing that I was me because of my mind, will, and emotions. Just me. The only thing that I had lost was my physical body. Yet I had the appearance of a physical body within a spiritual body. I do not know how to explain it. Then I realized that was why my hand could go through my face. I was a spiritual being of light yet clothed with immortality, with a heavenly one, you know? So I kept moving down. Another wave of light hit, total joy.

RANDY: I am looking at you, Shaun, and I am thinking Ian and I have had these experiences of otherworldly things. What is your take on this? Because right now we have gone from hell to Heaven, right?

SHAUN: Randy, I always feel like you are reliving your own experience in Heaven when our guests share their stories. The thing that has come to mind as Ian has been sharing is that it is like he was experiencing some of the fruits of the Spirit but in their extreme fullness. So many of the people we have talked to have shared about being immersed in God's love and having a sensory overload. Now I do not mean that with a negative connotation. It is like they are experiencing something in total completeness, an ultimate level of perfect fullness. That is what we have heard from nearly everybody who has shared an afterlife story with us.

IAN: Shaun, you are right. It was an overwhelming experience. There was this comfort that just enveloped me. It was everything you have been looking for in your entire existence. The peace of mind I felt at that moment has not left me in over 40 years. Then there was joy. It was not a joy that I used to get from getting wasted or when I was just being an idiot. It was an eternal joy that brought strength to your entire inner being. It was like your entire being had been waiting for this encounter all your life. I knew that wherever I was going, it could only get better. Suddenly I found myself coming out of the tunnel of light. I remember reading later that Jesus said small and narrow is the way, few find it, and no unclean thing can travel down it. I came out of this into a kingdom of light. The enormity would be as though you had now arrived at the center of the universe.

The tunnel made it look incredibly small. Now I had unrestricted access to a radiance that filled the heavens. I thought star systems and the entire universe must take their energy from this light. What was it? Was that just energy of good or was there something or someone in this radiance? As I was pondering this to myself, a person inside the light responded—the same person who led me through the Lord's Prayer, the same person who spoke to me on the beach. He said, "Ian, do you wish to return?" How did he know my name? There was a person there. Return where? So of course I turned back. Here was the tunnel dissipating back into darkness. I was going darkness, hospital bed…

Have I died? Has it transpired that I have left my form, moved through a valley of darkness, up a tunnel of light, and I am standing before a person who holds the radiance and glory of the universe around him? Is this real or am I lying in a hospital bed comatose in an NDE, near-death? My mind was playing tricks on me. It had endorphins. There was starvation of oxygen. I can give you all the clinical and intellectual arguments for it. And I could rationally walk through what was happening: *Am I lying in a near-death state, in a hospital with my eyes shut, hallucinating with endorphins and starvation oxygen? Is this a euphoric effect or am I dead, standing before a being of light, out of my body, and this is reality?*

RANDY: So we know in hindsight that it was the latter, that your brain was actually dead.

IAN: Correct. See this is the trouble: we rely a lot upon our so-called brain, but if you have a heart transplant, the mind is not just in the head. You can get the thoughts of a person when you move a heart to another body, so it is out of the heart. God looks at the heart. The heart reflects the true person. And I am not even talking about a physical heart. I am talking about the spirit of a man. So, the fact that you have a mind, will, and emotions, which I was going through, all of these, I was emotionally feeling love, peace, joy, all this stuff. I was able to cognitively think and rationally understand my position where I could be, and I could make a choice. I believe the Jews got it right: when a man dies, his spirit, his person leaves. The Greeks tried to break it up into body, soul, and spirit. I was out of my body. The same person who could think, feel, and rationalize in a physical body was now able to do the same. It was me, not separated, some part of me sleeping somewhere, talking and in front of a being of light.

SHAUN: The being of light whose voice had been leading you on this journey. Did you finally realize who it was?

IAN: I knew that whoever that was, there was nothing like Him in the entire universe. I assumed that this was God almighty.

Who that might be I could not see because of the radiance and the glory shining. So I just responded and said, "Look, if I am dead, if I am out of my physical body, I wish to return." He then responded, saying, "Ian, if you return, you must see in a new light." He qualified it. Light. See the light. I am seeing the light. This is where? Where else could you see? I have heard about people being enlightened. I have heard about people who have seen this light, that light, strobe lights. Who knows? I said, "Are you the true light?" That was my immediate response. He said, "Ian, God is light, and in Him, there is no darkness at all" [see 1 John 1:5]. I had no idea He was quoting Scripture because I had never read the Bible, but He was quoting something.

And as He spoke it, it appeared like I had seen the Lord's Prayer and like words of light. It was as though His word was coming out as words of light. Words were coming out and I could read what He was saying. So I could capture the essence of it. God is light in whom there is no darkness at all. I thought, *Well, I have just come from darkness and the men called it hell, hades.* I did not believe in it. I thought that was just to scare people. I thought hell was just a thing that people were frightened of. That was why they believed in religion. So I was going, *Well, there is a hell and it's darkness. God is light. Well, I have not believed in God and all I am seeing is someone surrounded by a light that fills the universe and it says that in Him, there is no darkness at all.*

So I stood there trying to look for darkness because there is always a shadow. So I looked behind me. To my amazement, I could see the light from His presence shining through my spiritual body of light and of course casting no shadow; as Scripture says, there is no shadow or shifting in the Lord. I read this later when I read the Bible. I had not had access to this, but it is true. All His Word is true. His Word is truth. God is light. In Him, there is no darkness at all. Yet Psalm 91 says, in the shadow of His wings. Well, if God has no shadows, then everything in His wings is only light. So I was standing there putting it together and going, *That must be what is called almighty God.*

I then reconciled the teaching of Buddhism and Taoism, which tries to put yin and yang in a circle of life. They made light and darkness equal and opposite. I had believed some of this. On my surfboard, I had town and country stickers with this symbol on them. And of course I was now realizing that that was not true. Light and darkness are not equal and opposite. You cannot have darkness amid light, which they have in the symbol. I was in a realm where light and darkness were separated and light would always overpower darkness. So I was getting a visual. I was getting false teaching obliterated from my mind; my esoteric New Age mind had just been shattered in seconds. I was then realizing that if He knew my name, knew my thoughts, knew before I even spoke the intention of my heart, then nothing was hidden from Him. Someone had made a dreadful mistake and beamed the wrong man up.

I should not have been in the presence of almighty God. I should crawl under some rock and judge myself back to hell before someone figured out the mistake. So, in my self-judgment, I began to feel exposed. So I began to move back toward the darkness to self-judge. As I moved back from the light, radiant waves of light penetrated out. I watched them come toward me, just like I had seen them come up the tunnel. I thought, *Oh, here it comes. The wrath, the judgment and anger of God. I will be catapulted back into the pits of hell.* But as this light hit me, instead of anger and judgment, I experienced unconditional love and acceptance. My gosh, I do not know how to explain it. My whole being was tingling with this liquid light that was giving off an emotion called love. People often ask, "How do you know it was love?" I say, "Man, I knew what love, sex, and passion were. This was pure. I could feel love from my mum that had a purity with no strings attached. This love had no strings attached. This was undeserved, unexpected, and unexplainable, but it was incredibly healing."

Wave after wave of love hit me. I said, "God, I have broken Your commandments. I have cursed You. I have slept around." So I told Him more of my sins because perhaps He didn't know. I thought there was no use getting in there and then being kicked out later. As I told Him all the stuff I had done wrong, His love intensified to the point I burst into tears and wept profusely. I had not wept like that since I was a 12-year-old boy.

Fourteen years later, I was a 26-year-old who was bawling his eyes out. People wonder how you can do that when you have no body, but something inside was weeping and love was filling me up. Shame and guilt were going. I then opened my eyes. I was encased in two to three feet of pure white light, radiance, and glory. Unbelievable love. And God said, "Son, in that ambulance, when you prayed, I did not forgive some of your sins. I forgave all of them." All my sins had been washed away. What can wash away my sins? Nothing but the blood of Jesus. Though my sins be scarlet red, He can make them as white as snow. Isn't that incredible grace? That is the heart of God. His love covers a multitude of sins. His love takes the deepest, filthiest sin and casts it into a sea of forgetfulness. He cleanses a man, no matter how filthy and messed up, and makes him clean in a second by the power of repentance. Without repentance, you will not have forgiveness. You must repent.

RANDY: Ian, we have had people message us, saying, "I do not want to experience hell." They are already believers in Jesus as their Lord and Savior but they fear that they will have to go through hell to get to Heaven. You were not a believer going into your experience and it was in the ambulance that you said yes to Jesus. That is when you made that confession and became a believer. So, at some point between accepting Christ and not having Him, there was the darkness and the hell experience. And then having received Him, the Heaven experience.

IAN: I asked God later, "What did You show me through that valley?" He said, "Well, Ian, nothing can separate us, but I wanted to show you what hell is like because you need to warn people. You need to tell them." I asked, "Will most people who love You go there?" He said, "No, they'll go straight into the light." And I have met tens of thousands of people who believe this. I believe the next time I die I will not go anywhere near that darkness. It will be straight into the realm of glory. And when you watch someone who loves the Lord die, you will see their face light up. They look past their loved ones and family as the king of glory is coming for them. Either the angel of the Lord or the Lord Himself, the light of the world, will come and step into their dimension and usher them straight into radiance.

I believe what God showed me of the true kingdom of darkness is incredibly important—not to be afraid of it because what can separate us from God, life, death, principality, power? Can lucifer separate us from God's love? No, the entire world lies in the power of evil and darkness anyhow. So you do not have to go to hell to figure it out. Just stay around Earth long enough. The days we live in are so dark and twisted that you are going to have to have faith in Christ, even amid trials, even amid tribulation, even while suffering, and it can purify and refine your spirit. There is a perfect love that casts out all fear. There is no fear in my body.

RANDY: Isn't that interesting, Shaun, that the experience of hell that Ian had, he is now proclaiming to others that the Lord was showing him that for a reason? And what do you think, Shaun, would be that reason? We have talked to a couple of people, such as Karina Ferrigno Martinez, who said she experienced satan, and Howard Storm, who said he experienced hell. What do you think is going on in these different experiences? Some people have gone directly into Heaven and others have had a brush with hell.

SHAUN: I feel the reality is that God gives experiences on both sides, so to speak, because that's part of the story that needs to be told. There is a literal hell where there is torment, weeping, and gnashing of teeth. We must talk about that too, let people know that there is a final destination and it is to one place or the other. In so many of the stories we have heard, people are rescued out of that darkness by Jesus or by angels. As we have seen, it varies from experience to experience.

Ian, a lot of people want to know how Jesus looked, to get some idea of His physical appearance. I would like to hear about His voice. If you can put it into words, what were the qualities of the voice that you heard and what rose inside you as that voice was communicating with you?

IAN: It was remarkably familiar and soothing. It was fatherly, like a voice you know well, but you realize it is not your voice. Out of the abundance of the heart, the mouth speaks. So you can hear the heart of the person who is speaking to you, and it is only for good. And God is good. I stood there weeping and surrounded by this light. And I wanted to see Him. I thought, *I am so close.* I now understand why all men fall short of the glory of God because the radiance around me was like a glowworm or a firefly, a little dot of insignificance. But it was surprisingly good for me. And the light that surrounded the Lord was the glory that filled the heavens.

The Scriptures say that the light's so bright, you will not need the light of the sun, the moon, or the stars. Can you imagine a radiance around a person that eclipses the sun? And the Scriptures also tell us about the Holy Spirit. It gives the fruits of love, peace, and joy. The Holy Spirit glorifies the Son. So I now know it was the third person of the Holy Spirit. It was His presence. He comes as light. He comes as radiance, fire, oil, all that stuff. He was glorifying the Son. I said, "Could I come in to see Him face to face? See Him speaking to me?" And I waited, but nothing. So I walked into this incredible light. It was like veils. I could then sense the light was healing my broken heart; this light was going deeper. My heart of hearts was being healed as I was weeping but feeling happy.

Next, I watched the light get brighter and brighter. And suddenly the veils of light that were surrounding Him began to part and I looked up. I was overwhelmed. Here was someone, arms outstretched, twenty to thirty feet away from me. And I immediately knew that was God. The robes He was wearing were robes of light made up of this incredible cloud of glory. He had shimmering garments of light, but they were white like monks' robes. And when I looked at His face, I saw His hair was pure white. That is what shook me. I did not know what to think. Is that Jesus? I had never seen Jesus with white hair, but His hair was shoulder-length, pure white.

And when I looked at His face, that was where the source of all the light in the universe was coming from. It was His countenance. It was so bright. It eclipsed every light I had seen to this point. It was seven to ten times brighter. When I looked directly at it, the light did not hurt my face. But I could sense that if He spoke, He could speak into existence galaxies and constellations. It was like looking into eternity within eternity within His countenance. So the fall of man, the face of God. I remember when a messianic Jewish friend gave me a Bible to read, I treasured it. I got to the end and read Revelation 1:13-18: His head and His hair were white like wool, like snow. He said, "I was dead but behold I am alive forevermore. I hold the keys of death and hades. I am the Alpha and the Omega."

And His face it says shone like the sun at full strength. So, when I read that, I just fell out. I thought, *That was written 2,000 years ago. This is John, the beloved, who Jesus said, "Take out, look after my mum, Mary."* You know what I mean? Here, he sees Jesus in His supernatural, glorified, resurrected form. And I have the privilege to be standing before the Son of God with arms of love reaching out. So I walked closer to Him, captivated by the beauty of it, and I experienced light emanating from His face and instant purity. My entire being felt the innocence of childhood restored as though His purity had been imparted into me. You cannot make yourself pure or forgive yourself. Only God can cleanse you of all your sins with His blood.

As I got closer, more light emanated out holiness, a very, very abstract word. I had never met anyone holy. Here the holiness of God filled me and I felt pure, holy, forgiven, loved, full of peace, full of joy, full of comfort, and a broken heart healed. I came right up to experience His presence and He began to move as though He wanted to show me more. But why couldn't I see His face? Why hadn't He unveiled His face to me? I did not know that no man looks upon the face of God and lives. Even Moses could not see it. But He moved like He was a door of radiance and light. As He moved, directly behind Him I could see a whole new dimension opening of grass and fields. I could see flowers. The radiance that was emanating across Jesus's countenance and entire being was emanating across this entire planet.

It was like a new Earth in front of me. I was getting words: Garden of Eden, paradise. Why hadn't I been born there in the first place? It was like I was looking at a parallel universe in time and space. It was like the matrix, like there was a totally new Earth. I was thinking that Heaven was supposed to be full of clouds with people wearing robes and walking around with little fat Italian babies, firing arrows, and Morgan Freeman swinging the pearly gates. No one had told me that God created a new Earth. And then I saw a crystal-clear river and heard the Lord saying I have a new Heaven, a new Earth, and a river of life. I could see trees—not just one tree, but trees of life. I looked up and I could see the new heavens. I was amazed. And I was assuming that above that was the new Jerusalem, the city of God, the bride of Christ. I was looking at the new Earth and was captivated by it.

I knew I was home. And Jesus came right back in front of me. The door into eternity closed. I had just had a glimpse. He said, "Ian, now you have seen. Do you want to stay here or do you wish to return?" What a choice! I said, "Stay here." No one wanted me to go back. Who would be dumb enough to go back? I had just had the love of God, who had called me by the name He had given. And you have set before you paradise without sin, without tears, without war, and without hatred. I said, "I have nothing to go back for." He did not move. I said, "No one loves me. No one back there. No children. I am not married. Please let me stay." He did not move. So, I looked back to say goodbye cruel world and this is what hit me. I saw a vision of my mum.

I had just told God that no one loved me, that there was no one to go back for. And here I was confronted with Mum, who was still praying for me alive on the earth. And I had been given the choice to go in. How would that impact my mother? She would have no idea that I had prayed. She would have no diary, no paramedic, no doctor, and no friend who could tell her this boy had turned his life around and was now a follower of God. There was no reference to it. I did it in an ambulance. No one heard me praying. It was done in my heart. I thought this would cripple my mother's faith and destroy her. Had I not seen her, I would not be standing here. Had I not been encouraged by her to pray, I would not have made that prayer. Had she not been interceding for me, would I have seen the Lord and called out? No. She could not repent for me. She could not pray for me, but she could pray for me to the point where I made that decision, where I called upon the name of the Lord. And I said, "I must go back to tell my mum that what she believes in is real. I must go back. I cannot live another selfish day of my life, where I just live for me. It would be ultimate selfishness to come in here without going back to tell my mother that what she believes in is real. There is a heaven. There is a hell. There is a risen Savior. It's all true. It's all true." No emotion. And I looked back and Jesus said, "Ian, if you return, you must see things in a new light." I understood. I would need to see from

His heavenly eternal perspective through eyes of love, not with all my bitterness and judgments, but from eyes of love. I had been so flipping arrogant and proud, but now I would have to see from humility, kindness, and gentleness what He had shown me. I would have to see from His eyes and His perspective, from an eternal, not an earthly, perspective.

When Jesus comes into you, Christ in you, you cannot help but be changed. That exchange—you give your heart to Him because you love Him. He gives His heart to you and He gives you His perspective on life. And it is an eternal perspective. I looked back and next to my mom appeared my dad, my brother, my sister, and millions of other people, a sea of humanity. I said, "God, why do You show me all these other people? I only know my immediate family." He said, "Ian, because most will not step foot inside a church any longer to hear My name. I want you to go back, tell them what you have seen." I said, "But, God, they will not believe me. They will not believe what I have seen. And I do not even know if I love these people." He said, "Ian, I love them. I desire all of them to come to know Me."

I said, "Well, I do not understand that kind of love. I can say I love my mom. I can go back for her. How do I go back down the tunnel into darkness and back into my physical body?" He said, "Ian, tilt your head, open your eye and see." And in a second I was back in my body, tilting my head, opening my eye to find that I was no longer in the emergency room. I was in the mortuary on a slab with a different doctor holding my foot with a scalpel, freaking out as this corpse came alive right in front of him.

Both of us were terrified. God then spoke, saying, "I have just given your life back." I said, "God, if that's true, can I look out the other eye?" So I rolled my head to the right and to the left and that doctor was spinning out of his tree. Three of the nurses had followed me from the emergency room down to the morgue. They see me and as my corpse moves, they freak out and bash into each other. I thought, *Well, this is not someone coming out of a coma. This is not someone coming out of a near-death experience. They are treating me like I am a dead piece of meat.* I potentially could have been dead. I looked back at the doctor. He dropped my foot and wanted to run. He said, "You have been dead for 20 minutes, son. We have done nothing to bring you back." I can see him almost urging me to tell him what I have seen. I thought, *My God, if I tell him I have seen the Lord, they will fill me up with Prozac and send me off to a mental asylum.*

My next thought was, *God, please heal me. I can feel nothing from the neck down. I have been dead for 20 minutes. I could be on a machine for the rest of my life. Please heal me or take me back to*

Heaven. Power went through me like electricity and within three or four hours, my entire body was supernaturally healed. I believe in the resurrection power of Christ and His healing presence. The next day I walked out of the hospital completely healed.

SHAUN: Next, Ian, I want to get into what happened after you left the hospital. You woke up in the morgue, you freaked out the doctors, and your body got hit with the electricity of God. You were dead. There was no earthly reason you should not have stayed dead. How complete was the healing you experienced and how soon was it until you left the hospital?

IAN: I went to sleep that night. The next day the fisherman found me. The next day I woke up to find Simone, whom I had been diving with, looking through the window, seeing that I was alive. He was freaking out, thinking that I was a spirit. He was trying to figure out if I was real. And I was trying to tell him and he said, "Come with us. We go home." And I was thinking, *Well, the doctors need to do some more checks, more tests or something.* He said, "No, no. You look all right, man. Look at you." So I stood up and thought, *Oh gosh, I can stand. Okay. I can walk.* I had nurses and doctors trying to stop me as we walked out of the hospital and jumped into the taxi with our other Creole friends, who were spinning out, man. They said, "Whoa, look at your arm, show." It had marks all over it.

We went back into the village that night. I went to sleep and woke up as though something had spooked me. Something was freaking me out. I was deeply at peace, but my body was shivering. I rolled over and looked out the window and saw seven people gawking at me. I thought, *Why have we got people flipping, coming to see the blinking jellyfish, whatever, and why are they staring and lurking outside my bedroom?* But then as I looked, I realized that they had a human form but they were shadowed, dark, spiritual beings. When I looked at their eyes, I could see their eyes did not have round pupils. They were slits like you would see on a serpent.

And I was thinking, *What the heck is that?* And then as I looked at them, they spoke to me and said, "You are ours and we are coming home." I was thinking, *You must be flipping joking, coming home?* I had no point of reference for when Jesus said an unclean spirit goes out of a man and finds six or seven worse in a dry, barren place and tries to come back into the house that has been swept clean so they can try to inhabit it. At that moment I was having a firsthand introduction to spiritual warfare 501, you know, instantly. I was seeing with my eyes that were now open to the supernatural and the spiritual realm. I was in a village that was full of voodoo. I had been places where they do evil things; I could sometimes feel it, but I had never seen it. It was much scarier when you think that you potentially had one of those evil things inside of you.

But of course, when you die, your spirit leaves. Why hang around the corpse? Go find some other poor soul. The Scriptures say they seek a place of rest. I turned the lights on and started freaking out. I wondered if I was going mental. Was I seeing the bogeyman? This seemed so loony tunes. I got to the point where I was sitting on the ground, thinking I had nearly snapped, when God said, "Son, pray the Lord's Prayer."

I could not fully remember it, so I walked through my previous experience and thought of the part of the Lord's Prayer where it says, "Deliver us from evil." God said, "Pray, deliver us from evil." So I said, "Now wait, God, I have a bunch of evil. I do not know where the heck they came from, but they are certainly attentive toward me. I do not know what I have done or what I have said, but, God, can you deliver me from the evil that is outside my window? That is just ominous." I finished praying the whole Lord's Prayer. I walked through the entire testimony. I remembered the whole thing, and God said, "Okay, son, now you have prayed. Turn the lights out and go to sleep." I responded, "God, that is easy for You to say; You are up there. I am down here. And I have a pack of whatever they are outside my window. You must be joking." I sat there and contemplated. I thought, *Well, the prayer worked last night. I mean, I went to Heaven. I saw God. Well, why not? Why not? God's got power over evil.* I decided to turn the lights out and wait to see if they would come back. They did not come back. I realized there was power in the Lord's Prayer.

So I got up in the morning and wandered down to the kitchen. My Aussie and New Zealand roommates were talking to each other. As they were talking, I could hear four conversations. I could hear what they were saying out of their mouths, but I could also hear what they were thinking about each other. It was not very nice. And as I was observing this, I asked God what this was all about. God responded, "You are seeing people in a new light. You can hear the heart's intent inside of a person." One of them turned to me and I could hear what he thought about me. That was a little bit unnerving, and I am not referring to what was coming out of his mouth. So I ducked off and went down to the bedroom and hid for a moment. Thank God for peace and quiet. This sort of thing could drive a person crazy. If you start seeing in the spirit realm, then you start seeing the intent of people's hearts. I wondered how this all worked.

Later that evening I was woken up in the middle of the night. There were three spiritual entities, which I can only understand to be demons from the Bible, standing in the shape of a human form. If you think they were once angels, I am sure they had some angelic body. Now God had destroyed it. I think Ezekiel 28:18 says that God consumed lucifer and the angelic bodies with fire. So that's spiritual darkness because we do not fight against flesh and blood. So I was now seeing spiritual beings of darkness, trying to assail me. That freaked me out, so I turned the lights on.

For some reason, they hated the light. I sat down and went through the same experience, and God said, "The Lord's Prayer saved your life. Deliver us from evil—pray it again." Bam! I prayed and they were gone. So the next night I woke up. There was a girl I had been trying to move on, a beautiful young Creole girl. She said, "Hey, I want to talk to you." I was thinking, *No, I am not interested in girls. Just leave me alone.* She said, "I have got to talk to you. It's so important." I walked around the side of the house and opened the door. And here was this young girl and the red spiritual entities that I had seen out of their physical bodies. One of them was inside her. I could see it inside her eyes. She held the door. I could not shut it. Her voice had changed.

So I had this woman speaking with a man's voice and I was thinking, *That is the thing that is in her. What the heck?* And it said, "You are coming with us tonight." I could not physically shut the door. I could not budge it. I could hear someone or something crawling on the edge of the house. And I went, *God, help me!* The next minute my hand lifted and I said, "In Jesus's name." I thought, *Did I just say that?* And then an invisible fist hit this girl on the chest. Her physical body was thrown through the air and onto the ground. I was going, *This is madness!* "Jesus" had been a swear word. Now that word had power. I wondered what the heck was going on. That woman had some evil thing in her. She was demonized. I had heard about demonized people going into trances, walking on fire, and hanging from meat hooks. I had seen some of that stuff.

I was beginning to connect the dots and realized this woman must be involved in voodoo. Who knew what she was involved in or what spirit she had gotten involved with. Her body moved like a snake, trying to lunge toward me. I slammed the door shut and was freaking out. I wondered what I had done to cause these spiritual beings to want to take me out. God said, "Well, your sin will find you out: you were willing to try to sleep with that girl. And in this world, if you sleep with one of the local girls, you either marry them or the brothers will kill you."

That must have been right. I had seen that happen in Thailand. I had seen that in various parts of the world. You touch the locals and you are in trouble, but normally you get away with it when you are a sinner like me. Now, I had just seen God. I was praying every day. The Bible says, let there be no foothold, no sin. That puts the fear of God in most Christians. Do not muck around, you know? So I was standing there thinking I needed to get out of this country.

The next night I saw a spear come through the window. Her boyfriend and brothers were trying to kill me where I slept. I shined the torchlight at them and their eyes were red. And now I had three men with red eyes and the girl whose eyes were red outside my house. I realized that was where some of those flipping demons must have gone. For some reason, they were trying to kill me. And I of course had the name of Jesus and the power of the Lord's Prayer. I also had a bit of Irish in me, which is called McCormack—a family name that means no fear.

I now understood that the demons cowered back from the light and the prayers.

RANDY: Ian, we can be in two different places in the world. One person might be working in a factory and another person is vacationing on a mountaintop, but they are both part of the world. However, the experiences we have in that world on the other side of the veil are different. Each experience with God is something incredibly unique and reflective of how He wants to reveal Himself to us individually.

IAN: The Lord had shown me the kingdom of darkness and now I was realizing that that kingdom of darkness rules much of this world. By God's grace, I was able to get out and make it to Perth; I flew out of there. I met up with my brother and shared my testimony with him and it freaked him out. I slept in his best friend's bedroom, who was away in Nepal. In the middle of the night, I was attacked by these white-eyed spiritual entities. As I walked around, God showed me that they came out of a Buddha statue that was sitting on the fireplace. I wondered why the white-eyed demons had come out of that idol. It turned out his roommate was studying to be a Nepalese monk and was talking to some guru up in the mountains of Nepal. Previously I had thought Buddhism was quite harmless, but here I was finding that the idols have spiritual entities inside of them and the Bible calls them demons.

Next, I flew home to New Zealand. When I got home, I got a sense of another demonic attack. I said, "God, how do I get rid of them?" Do you know what He said? He told me to read the Bible. He had already told me in the plane; when I asked Him what had happened to me, He said, "You are a reborn Christian." I said, "I have heard of Catholics, I have heard of Baptists, but what is reborn?" He said, "When you prayed the Lord's Prayer in the ambulance, you were born again." And I said, "I do not understand all this." He said, "If you want to know, read a Bible." I said, "I do not have one. I have never read one." He said, "Your dad's got one." So I walked into the bedroom and asked my dad. Within six weeks I had read the entire Bible.

My mum started weeping when she walked in one day and saw me reading the Bible. She was so excited and she asked me what had happened. I told her and she burst into tears and told me how she had been praying. We gave each other a hug. She asked me to show her what I was reading. I showed her and she said, "Oh, in my church they do not get us to read much. It is usually the priest's job." I said, "Mum, it would be good if we started reading and studying the Bible."

My girlfriend took me to a church that had contemporary music. Their faces were shining. People were loving the Lord. Here I had a messianic dude come up behind me and ask me to his Bible study. He told me I needed to get baptized, both water baptized and baptized in the Spirit. This period of time was such an adventure. It was like the entire world was just full of God's presence. Although there was darkness, you just had to lift your eyes and let the light and glory of God fill you. That is our greatest protection, to be in the realm of God's presence. In light darkness must flee and it is dispelled by the love of God. I love Him and cannot wait to go back.

RANDY: Amen. Amen.

SHAUN: Ian, I feel like you have one of the most unique getting-pushed-into-deliverance-ministry sort of stories. Thank you for sharing those different encounters. I am curious, have demonic manifestations and deliverance ministry always been a core part of your ministry through the years?

IAN: I do not go looking for them. Some people get all preoccupied. The whole key is to focus on the open Heaven and the glory of God. This is your full armor of light. The greatest place to fight is from a heavenly perspective, not an earthly one. When demons do come across your path, sometimes it is sickness. That person needs a miracle. Sometimes they need counseling because they have a broken heart. Sometimes they simply need an arm of comfort and love; they just need to be held. Other times there is a spiritual entity, depending on whether they have been in the occult or witchcraft or some other form of seeking truth. Sometimes they have encountered a demon through astral travel or yoga. They have invited entities into them, which become things that need to go out. And we have power in the name of Jesus to heal the sick, cast out demons, and to set captives free.

Jesus continually saw what was needed. Do they need food? Feed them. Do they need to be healed? Heal them. Do they need to come and just see His glory and be loved back to life? All of it is helpful to make the body, soul, and spirit entire and complete. So we need to bring the whole gospel, which is that God is working in every area of our being. For some people, great deliverance can come through forgiveness, by them forgiving others. Great deliverance can come. If you get to the root, the enemy has no hold. I have seen more deliverance done by ministering to the heart of people and for them working through forgiving others than being healed by God. You remove the legal right through unforgiveness and bitterness and through the power of the Holy Spirit. They depart without you even having to address them. Sometimes you do have to confront them and walk through a complete demonic confrontation, but we try not to get there. There are other ways to get to the soul and get to the spirit of that person.

RANDY: You said something interesting, Ian, "the legal right"? We do not oftentimes think of the legality of God's way in that the Lord's Prayer, which you have referenced, says. The second part of that is forgiveness. I forgive; I ask forgiveness. Forgive me, Lord, of my trespasses, as I forgive those who have trespassed against me. So that is the release of that?

IAN: It is the key, but then they must be willing to receive the healing. So, when you are forgiven, it does not mean you are healed. It gives the ability. Once you forgive others, it does not mean by forgiving them you are saying what they did was right. Even if what they did was evil and demonically inspired, if you release that forgiveness, God then can come in and heal your broken heart, restore holiness, restore purity, restore dignity, and take the shame away. That has been my direct experience. He will make all of that new again. He can bring you back as if you have never had sex before in your life, never been abused, and never been hurt. God can restore you back to childlike innocence through a spirit of adoption and through His incredibly healing love. This is powerful. I find a lot of people say they are forgiven, but when I ask, "But have you been healed?" they say, "No, but I keep forgiving." I tell them, "No, you got it right the first time." People need to come into a place where the love of God will, by the Spirit, touch and heal their inner man, because out of that comes the wellspring of life. People cannot survive with a broken heart.

STORIES OF HEAVEN AND THE AFTERLIFE

RANDY: Yes. And then the third part of that is, lead me not into temptation but deliver me from evil—so there comes the forgiveness, part of the cleansing of unrighteousness; and then, protect me from entering into sin or temptation.

IAN: Absolutely. That is right. And walk in the light as He is in the light. Put your hands in the hands of the Master. Allow Him to surround you by His radiance and glory and be changed in the inner man from glory to glory. Allow Him to lift you up into heavenly places daily. You are of no earthly use unless you get seated up with Him and start being caught up. Many people talk about gold coming down, but in my experience, most of my real encounters as a Christian are being caught up into the throne room, caught up into the manifest presence of God, caught up into the third heaven. And this is where you get revelation. This is where you get encounter. This is where you get heavenly perspective. And that's exactly what John the beloved had on the isle of Patmos in the spirit. On the Lord's Day, he was caught up instantly, and though he is still alive, he sees Jesus glorified.

Then John sees the door open and sees the throne room and sees the elders and living creatures before him. And he encounters God the Father; he sees Jesus glorified and he is still alive. That is why it is a revelation of Jesus Christ. Most people read it as a revelation of the antichrist. No, it is a revelation of Jesus Christ.

That is why that encounter must be a norm of Christianity. We are in the world but not of it. We are to be touched by an open heaven and the glory realm. You must see the glory of God daily to be changed from glory to glory. Moses saw it and his countenance showed it. If the inner man has been transformed, the outer countenance will have the shining radiance of one who has met with Jesus.

SHAUN: Ian, when people encounter these afterlife stories, they tend to be attracted to fantastical elements like seeing God's glory, seeing Heaven, or seeing Jesus. What is the key takeaway you want every person to discover when they encounter your story?

IAN: I think the greatest, and the one that has had the greatest impact on my life, is the love of God. Perfect love casts out all fear. Love will remain. We love because He first loved us. So you can have resurrection power, you can see glory, you can see radiance, but the key is that God is love and all of us are looking for that. Love is the greatest. We will be changed when the God of the universe comes and touches us with His divine, romantic love—the kind of love that changes you forever. That is the key for me. Everything else is extraordinary, but the person of Christ, He is the living word of God made flesh. I beheld His glory. I fell in love with the person of Jesus and I love Him because He first loved me back to life.

I did not have the capacity to know how to respond to that until He first loved and healed me. His love prepared me to meet Him face to face. That is the hallmark of everything that I know. I hope people get the manifest love, the tangible love, that can come from God to them. This will make you secure. This will be an anchor to your soul. This will be the hallmark of everything. The security of His acceptance and love for you will take all striving and performance away. It will bring you to a place of rest.

RANDY: This whole story came from a man who was an atheist but is now a believer in Jesus Christ, involved in deliverance from demons and in preaching the truth of the gospel. That is a miracle. As we talk about visiting Heaven and hell with people who have been there, it confirms the reality of Heaven and hell and gives us certainty about who God is. What a profound takeaway!

REFLECTIONS ON IAN McCORMACK'S EXPERIENCE

RANDY: Ian is the second person with whom Shaun and I have spoken who credited the prayers of his mother for his salvation. There is a pattern we are witnessing for those who died without knowing Jesus as their Savior, which is an exposure to hell, as with Ian, and an acknowledgment of God's presence because of someone's intercessory prayer or an earnest desire to know the truth. God hears the prayers of His children. I know that in my case people were praying for me after I died and I heard those prayers in Heaven. This should give hope to those who have prayed for their loved ones who have since died. While many with whom we have spoken (like Ian) testify of hell as a real and wretched place, as they were haunted by demons, God listens and responds to the prayers of His saints. In Ian's case, he saw the written Word of God before encountering Jesus, and the Bible is imprinted upon his heart today, having ministered for decades.

Like several we have interviewed, Ian looked through a tunnel; only in Ian's case God showed him a vision of his family and thousands of other people. He asked God why he was being shown all of these people, and God told Ian that if he did not return, then many of these people would not get a chance to hear about God. This directly correlates with a common reason for the return of those of us who died, met God in Heaven, and were returned for the purpose of declaring the truth of God and Heaven. God is releasing stories like Ian's as a testimony of the truth of Jesus and His resurrection power.

SHAUN: There are three things that really stuck out to me from Ian's story.

First is Ian's miraculous recovery after being stung by five box jellyfish. He should have been dead within five to ten minutes. There wasn't anything the doctors did to bring him back that would explain why he suddenly woke up in the morgue. On top of that, when you consider his miraculous full healing and that he walked out of the hospital the next day, the only explanation is the power of God.

Second, as Randy mentions above, is the prayers of Ian's mother and how they were one of the key forces behind his salvation experience. We have encountered numerous people in our NDE and afterlife interviews who have told us that but for the prayers of their parents, they would be in hell. These accounts concretely reinforce the importance and power of prayer and help us to see just how much Heaven responds when we pray.

Last, I want to comment about Ian's experience of seeing and experiencing demonic entities shortly after he returned from Heaven. Many of the people Randy and I have talked to share that after they returned to Earth, they feel like they always have one foot in Heaven and one on Earth. Others talk about having a heightened sense of spiritual awareness and insight. From my perspective, it seems that when people experience Heaven, it is common for a seer or prophetic gifting to be awakened in them. As Ian shared in our conversation, deliverance ministry has been a normal part of his experience in the years following his time in Heaven.

FIND OUT MORE

If you would like to encounter more of Ian McCormack's story, be sure to check out the 2014 film *The Perfect* Wave, which tells his story. You can also connect with Ian at aglimpseof eternity.org.

CHAPTER 3

FROM HELL TO HEAVEN, MAN DIES AND MEETS BOTH HITLER AND JESUS

MEET BRYAN MELVIN

Bryan Melvin, a self-described militant atheist, died after contracting cholera from drinking contaminated water at a construction site.

In this conversation, Randy and Shaun talk with Bryan about his time in Heaven and hell, especially focusing on the ongoing experiences of the people he saw who had been condemned to hell. He saw abusers, killers, and even a preacher. However, the most notable person Bryan saw is one of the most reviled men in all of history, Adolf Hitler. What Bryan saw will shock you, but know his story ends with redemption and hope.

INTERVIEW WITH BRYAN MELVIN

SHAUN: Bryan, let's start by having you give us some context, for your upbringing, faith exposure, and a bit about who you were before your near-death experience.

BRYAN: I grew up in a Southern Baptist Christian home. We were always made to go to church when I was little, but that ended as soon as I got old enough and started thinking for myself. I always say that the cartoon *Rocky and Bullwinkle* corrupted me because they had Sherman and the time machine and they would go back in time and talk about all of these Greek philosophers. I went to the library to find books on philosophy and started reading those. I got to the point that I just did not believe in God so much and fell away, bouncing between atheism and agnosticism, eventually becoming a full-blown militant atheist. That is my background.

RANDY: Next, tell us the circumstances that led up to your near-death experience.

BRYAN: I was an electrician working at a construction site in Tucson, Arizona. It was always hot there. On that day, the marquee on the bank across the street read 121 degrees. We always tried to get started super early in the morning so we could be done by noon or 1 p.m. at the latest. My supervisor had just gotten back from taking his family to Mexico. On the way back his car overheated, so he filled up the company thermos with pond and creek water from Mexico and brought it back in his truck.

In those days it was construction etiquette that if you ever walked by a truck and you saw a cooler, you could drink out of it because it was so hot. The first thermos I grabbed from the truck was empty. The one way in the back was full. I lifted this big five-gallon jug over my head and started drinking. Then I handed it to a coworker and I said, "Boy, this is warm." He took one little sip and spat it out. When he opened the top of the jug, it looked like Darwin soup. Have you ever seen algae-infested water? That is what I drank. It had little worm things swimming around in it that looked like flat spaghetti. The short story is that I drank contaminated water and contracted cholera and who knows what else.

SHAUN: Bryan, in terms of your body reacting to taking in that contaminated water, did you end up in the hospital? What were your surroundings as your body was declining?

BRYAN: My surroundings were, simply put, that I was a strong guy who was going to do things his own way. I took the medications of Jack Daniels and Wild Turkey, thinking that would kill whatever it was I drank. I joked about it the whole night. I did not go to the hospital right away and thought I could just take care of it myself.

I had a duplex apartment with a couple of roommates and we had been making plans to go up and fly over to the Grand

Canyon on the holiday weekend. I had a friend up there in Phoenix with a private plane. I fully expected to go along, but then I got sick.

The next day I went to work and suddenly it hit me fast. Let me warn you: if you ever have cholera, it comes out of both ends. I had a high fever and it felt like razor blades were cutting up my stomach and gastro-intestinal tract from the inside out. It was extremely painful. My friends still left on the Grand Canyon trip that Saturday and planned for a neighbor to check on me.

With cholera your body goes into shock from losing too many fluids. At that point, you temporarily feel great. The pain goes away. You can get up and walk around. I was telling the guys, "I am fine; it will pass. I am up and around. I am just a little tired. See you in the evening." I walked into the kitchen as they walked out of the house and got in the truck. I assured them they did not have to worry about me. I walked back into the kitchen and stood there at the window, trying to take a drink as they drove off.

Suddenly it hit me again and I collapsed on the floor like a ton of bricks, following the classic symptoms of cholera. I do not know how long I was on the floor, but I crawled back and managed to get into the bathroom before I passed out. Then

I crawled into my bedroom and somehow lifted myself up on the bed. I was lying on my bed, looking at my alarm clock, and trying to pet my German Shepherd dog at the same time. That was when something happened. It was like I took my last breath. I was not wearing my glasses, but as soon as that happened, I noticed I could see clearly across the room. That was odd because I am very nearsighted.

My clock was in front of me and showed that it was ten minutes before noon. I tried to pet my dog, but my hand went through him. I saw a hand come out of my own hand and go through my dog's chin. My dog started whimpering and crying. And then I began to float above my body. Let's just say I lost my atheism as soon as I started floating above my body, because I realized that I was still alive. In fact, I was more alive after I had left my body than I am right now. It's hard to explain, but that is how it felt.

RANDY: Many people describe when they transition into that initial out-of-body experience that they felt horrible because they were so sick, and then suddenly they felt better. You just said that you felt more alive after leaving your body. Was this your experience too?

BRYAN: That is exactly what happened. There was no more pain. I felt good and totally at peace, the most peace I had ever felt. I did not want to go back into that old body and go through all of this stuff. The next thing I knew, I went through the ceiling and passed the swamp cooler on the roof, and on up into what I would call a black void heading toward a light. Within that black void, I was drifting toward this light. I felt peaceful. It was the most joyous experience I had ever had. I felt love and compassion and heard this beautiful music. This music was in another language, but I could understand what was being sung. It was praising God. They were praising Him for the mysteries of the universe. And there I was floating there, getting a life review. I did not realize that I was headed toward a reckoning. If my neighbor would have found me at that moment and gotten me to the hospital and resuscitated me, I would have a vastly different testimony, because I would tell everybody to go to the light. I was up for a rude awakening and a reckoning just around the corner.

SHAUN: Bryan, keep going with the story. We cannot wait to hear what happened next.

BRYAN: What happened next was, I was going through this void and I was having this sense of love and compassion. When I got to where the light was getting bigger, I could see that it was coming from a person who was standing on a rock, and behind Him it opened and I could see a grand city, but then it got dark and I could see something else, but I could not make it out. I floated toward the rock. I landed feet first on the rock and the person who was on the rock was wearing a robe and light was coming from Him.

It was a brilliant light of many colors and shades. I cannot even explain this brilliant white light; it was phenomenal. It was coming from the person and He had His hands in His robe. When He took His hands out, it really got bright. Like I said earlier, I landed feet first before Him and then I fell down face first. Then somebody or something picked me up, even though I did not want to get up. I was right in front of Him. He had a hood on and I recognized who it was. It was Jesus! And I was facing a reckoning because what was being revealed to me at that moment was how I had gained everything that God had given me.

He loves us unconditionally. He makes the rain fall on the unjust. He makes sure the animals are fed. He takes care of things. He nurtures. He builds up. So, what did I do with it? I took advantage of everything. He gave me good parents. I lied to and betrayed them. He gave me friends. I lied to them, betraying and stabbing them in the back. I stole from people. I sold drugs to the church youth group. I was a corrupter of youth. I could see how the people who were at the skating party were getting whacked out on what I had sold them. I became one of the biggest drug pushers in the entire school and I knew nothing about drugs.

I had to make an image change really quickly and get involved in that scene just to cover myself. That was how I lied to myself and betrayed people. It was all revealed to me. The Lord showed me how I made life ugly, and when you make life ugly in a biblical sense, you transgress God's law. Most people do not understand that it is a royal law of love. It is loving God with all of your heart, mind, and soul and loving your neighbor as yourself.

God revealed to me how I took advantage of people, so I could not go up to the Lord and say, "You know, Lord, I had a crazy sign hit me on the head and that is why I acted crazy. I am just a victim of circumstance." There was nothing like that. I could not say anything. I saw how ugly I was on the inside. No matter my excuses, no matter how many good things I did, they did not cover up what I was like on the inside.

RANDY: Bryan, there are a couple of things I want to reflect on in terms of not being able to stand in the presence of the Lord. We have heard many people who have had near-death experiences say that when they get into the presence of God or encounter Jesus, they cannot do anything but be on their knees, bow, or be facedown in the presence of that level of holiness.

In terms of your life review, could you see the ways what you did impacted others? What was it like to see it from their vantage point?

BRYAN: It was more of a sensation of feeling what they felt. I could feel my parents' pain seeing me strung out on drugs and talking nonsensically. They knew it and they loved me, but they still knew I was stealing their money and doing this stuff. I saw how I made God feel too. It says that after you die comes judgment; well this is a judgment. You must face yourself. The real you is exposed. Whether you are a Christian or not, nobody is going to stand before Him thinking they are hot stuff and all justified. That will all be flushed down the proverbial commode. You are going to see what you are really like.

It was not pleasant. I never really answered the Lord. I wanted to, but I could not. I was flummoxed, like a deer in the headlights. You realize this is real and you wonder why you did not listen. I saw how good the Lord had been to me. He witnessed to me, He spared my life through multiple car wrecks, He saved me from being shot two times, and so much more.

SHAUN: Bryan, what happened following your life review?

BRYAN: Well, after that He said I would see a land unknown that is best forgotten but not to be left unseen. I remember those words. It was still an option to be decided, basically if I return or not to where I was standing. Then He said, "When you arrive at this place, say My name and My title." I understood that His name and title were Jesus Christ because I knew who He was. I was immediately picked up by a force and went to what would have been Jesus's left side toward a doorway that opened like a scroll.

I went through it and was cast into a tunnel-like vortex moving toward a yellowish dim light, a different type of light. I fell out of the sky and bounced on the ground. I stood up and thought I must be in hell. I remember when I was a kid, everyone talked about hell having fire and brimstone, devils, and the guy wearing tights with the pitchfork and wings and stuff. There was none of that.

I was sitting on a hill and there was a little valley with a house on the other side of it. Everything was brownish and dead-looking because it was so hot. The house was oddly like the house that I used to live in with my parents back in Virginia, but not quite; there was a difference. There was a dilapidated tree in the wrong place in the yard. It was where our driveway would have been. It was not the same house, but it was. I saw all that and then all these people came out of the house. Then more people came up out of the valley. It looked to me like they were coming to welcome me to paradise, slapping me on the back and everything. However, things just did not feel right.

I kept thinking that some of these people could not really be here because they were not dead. The people began to morph into other creatures right in front of me, trying to distract me. One even tried to appear as my mom, and I said, "You are not my mom. My mom's not dead. You are not dead." Then they all changed. I could see that their eyes were like alligator eyes with yellow irises. And suddenly I could see what they really looked like. That was when they all surrounded me and I started saying Jesus's name and title nonstop. I had permission. He gave me permission to say His name and title. That is the first thing that people need to realize.

He gave me permission to say His name in this place. When I said His name, they could not grab hold of me. They could not bite me, but they could push me and touch me. Being poked and prodded by these creatures was an odd sensation. The good news is that they were unable to do what they had originally been planning to do. One creature came forward out of the crowd, who I nicknamed lizard breath. In fact, I found a statue of this creature that was made near Loveland, Colorado. I saw it from a distance and told my brother-in-law, "That looks like the creature I saw." It is the best representation I ever saw of lizard breath.

So we walked over to it. It had a dinosaur or alligator-like tail, like it was reptilian, but his mouth was bigger. I could not tell you how many eyes he had because his breath was so foul that it would distort his face. He took me and he said, "Come, follow me, and I will give you half of my kingdom." Let me go back to the statue really quick. When I saw the statue, it was opening day for this place. This statue was in the African art section and it said this is the traveler who escorts people into the underworld. Talk about creepy. This was a total *Twilight Zone* moment for me.

SHAUN: So you have transitioned into this new space that looks parched and brown and you see what looks like the house you grew up in. One of the creatures comes forward, the traveler who escorts people into the underworld. Do you follow him? If so, where does he take you?

BRYAN: I started following him and we took a few steps towards the horizon. He stuck his hands into the horizon and ripped it open. He stepped up and out of this place and motioned for me to come. I did not know what to do, so I just followed him, because I did not want to stay there with those creatures. I came out of a cube or a cell and was standing on a wide dusty road. The Bible talks about chambers of death and it describes hell as a pit with a dungeon and cells. I was seeing the pit of hell but at the time I did not fully grasp what I was seeing. I was scared, but at the same time I also knew I deserved this place. I wanted to wake up but could not.

So I was standing there trying to process all of this and all I could do was follow this creature. He started pointing toward the road and all the things that were going on. I could see tornado vortexes dropping people off into the cells just like I had been. I also saw this wide dusty road with these gaggles of hideous-looking creatures. These demonic entities were escorting people along this road and delivering them to these cells. It was extremely hot, dry, and dusty. As Bill Wiese says, "It is so hot, your eyeballs are going to melt out of their sockets." The dirt of the place felt like I was walking on rotted flesh, but it was dusty. Very strange. I could see hot glowing rocks in various places and I could hear a roar of flame too. It all stank. It smelled so bad I could taste it.

I kept following this creature and he took me to the center of the road to a circular pit. The best way I can describe it would be a spiral staircase. The bricks were the cells and the cells were stacked six high and layered as a bricklayer does in a circle. Behind the first few cells, it opened into little V-shaped formations and little rooms the farther it went back. We walked over there and when I looked down, I saw a bottomless pit that went as far as I could see.

The creature told me this was a grand place. He motioned to me and I followed him back toward the cubes. When we got back over to the cubes, all I could do was just stare. We looked inside two of these cubes and I could see people inside of these cells. Somehow I was instantly granted knowledge of their life history. I knew how and when they got there.

I could see what was going on in the cell from my perspective, but I also could see from the perspective of the person inside the cell and what they were experiencing. This is exceedingly difficult to explain, but I could see it from both perspectives at the same time. So I was looking at this stuff transpiring and the people were experiencing just degrees of recompense just like the Bible says, payback for how they gamed the system, gamed God, and made life ugly. It all comes back to you. You are dwelling in a never-ending nightmare. That is what these people were experiencing and I saw a lot of people.

There was a professor writing on a blackboard. He had corrupted youth with his ideas. He never thought that there would be any payback for what he was teaching.

I walked to another cell and saw a minister who was not really a minister. He was looking to have his way with the young girls and ladies. He died during the Cane Patch Revival. As he sat inside his cell, he thought he was at a revival meeting, but nobody paid attention to him. The room was not filled with people; there were demons sitting on the chairs. All the props, including the chairs, were demons. When they got up and chased him out, they began beating him with a big black book. He thought he could run, but the inside of these cells were small. As he ran, the scenery would change, but I could see what was going on. It was like he was running on a treadmill, like what you saw inside the holodeck on *Star Trek: The Next Generation*. He was running and suddenly an entity came down through the roof of this place. He had cloven hooves with talons. He put his talons on the man's chest and laughed as he crushed the life out of him. Then it would begin all over again. Another scene would change and he continued reaping what he had sown.

RANDY: My father was in World War II fighting to free people from the control of Nazi Germany and Japan. When people are asked to identify the most evil person who has walked the earth in modern history, they tend to point to one specific individual. Many wonder if he could have been redeemed at the last moment, but you have an answer to that. Tell us what you saw.

BRYAN: To make a long story short, we came to a row of cells and I saw some Nazis, people who had committed horrible atrocities, and they were experiencing being shot and killed. I saw the man who was known as the blonde butcher. He orchestrated and laid the foundation for the final solution. He was killed in Czechoslovakia in 1942.

I walked to another place and there were all these entities around and I stopped and looked inside this one cell that looked like the inside of a furnace. Inside I saw Adolph Hitler. You could not mistake him. People do not realize the depth of the vile hatred that he had and how much he was involved in the occult. His powers of deception were acquired through Luciferianism, a religion practiced by the ancient Nordic pagans.

He was being gassed and cremated repeatedly. His flesh would be consumed, burned off by the flames, and then come back. I cannot explain it. He was feeling the pain, yet he was also getting violently angry.

RANDY: He was going through that same destruction that he put so many Jewish people through.

BRYAN: Yes. The part I saw was him experiencing the flames of the furnace, but I knew intuitively that he also experienced the gas chambers. He experienced being stripped. He experienced being raped. He experienced being buried alive. He endured all the atrocities that he put the Jewish people through.

RANDY: That was such a horrendous period in world history. When you saw Adolph Hitler, did he look like what he looked like in real life?

BRYAN: It was unmistakably him. He had his little mustache and everything. He looked like a picture I had seen of him from about 1945, where he was pinching some German kid soldier on the cheek. That guy survived the war and talked about that. He looked like that, but he was bent over. Some people say that he might have had Parkinson's, or Parkinson's that was induced by the drugs that he was being given. He was a drug addict. People do not know it, but it has come out that Dr. Morell gave him shots and some synthetic form of methamphetamine.

RANDY: He was reliving that same hellish experience that he put others through. And we can confirm certainly through your account that God is a God of justice.

SHAUN: So you are continuing to follow that creature down a path, deeper into hell. You have that knowing perspective that I have heard about from Ivan Tuttle, where you just know why they are there, what happened, the circumstances of their life. What was your journey out? How do you go from experiencing that to coming back into your body?

BRYAN: I followed the creature down several more levels. Each level we went down, the more the torments increased. Eventually, we came to a cell that was open and looked like it had a dentist's chair in it. This was how it was all supposed to end for me. This is where my cell would have been. Somehow I just knew that. This cell was a little larger than the other ones and it was open, meaning that the whole host of hell could come in and torment me. I realized that when the creature had said, "I offer you half of my kingdom," he was offering for half of the kingdom of hell to torment me. I was at my wits' end. This was the end and this was where I belonged. This was where I was going to spend my eternity. I understood that this was what I deserved. I had lost all hope. I wanted to wake up but could not.

Suddenly I felt a presence coming in behind me. As it got closer all of the entities scurried out of there and left. The ground was shaking and rocking with each footstep. At the moment I lost all hope, the presence came up behind me and lifted me up. That was when I recognized who it was because of His wrists, the bones pulled apart. Later I found out that Psalm 22 talks about somebody hanging on a cross, His bones pulled apart. At that moment, I realized that if I had been alive in New Testament times, I would have been the soldier driving the nails and I did not deserve to be rescued. When He picked me up, I felt the most incredible compassion I had ever felt in all of my life. I cried on His shoulder as we went back through this maze of stuff and came out on the wide dusty road.

We backtracked through all of the places I had been. This was Jesus carrying me. Years later I now know that Psalm 40 does not apply to me; it applies to anybody who has ever felt like they have been abandoned, but it applies even more to what Jesus went through prophetically than to me. So the imagery in what I went through is remarkably similar in that my feet were in miry clay, I had given up all hope, and Jesus rescued me when I deserved it not. And finally, when we returned to where it all began, He set my feet upon a rock, the same rock as when I entered.

I will not say everything that He said; I just cannot. He blew on me and He spoke to me thought to thought. He said, "Go in peace." Peace is exactly what I felt. I went back through the dark void, hearing the beautiful music, and feeling great again. I came through the ceiling and landed feet first. I landed in the same position I had died in. I could not breathe. When I looked at the clock, it was now ten to four. Now this next part is a bit hazy. I know I could not breathe. I do not know how the neighbor found me at all. The next thing I knew, I was standing outside and this guy was trying to hold me up and get me in his truck to rush me to the hospital. That was where I was diagnosed with cholera.

RANDY: Bryan, thank you for sharing your amazing near-death experience with us. In terms of following Jesus and understanding why you were sent back, did you come to understand that you have a purpose and call on this latter side of your life journey?

BRYAN: After I got out of the hospital, I was at home sitting on a beanbag chair and I said, "Jesus, I never want to go back to that awful place. Take me. I am Yours." That was my salvation prayer. As soon as I said that, I felt a cool breeze blow upon me and enter me. Keep in mind that I was in my duplex apartment in Tucson, Arizona, which only had a swamp cooler, and it had been between 114 and 121 degrees for several days. Given that context, you can understand why feeling that cool breeze was significant to me.

John chapter 3 has a special meaning to me where it says you are born from above, because that is where the breeze came from. It came from above, engulfed me, then it went inside of me. I haven't been the same since. My life took a 180-degree turn. It was a slow turn. It took me almost a year before I started going to church. After that, I was messed up and was having post-traumatic stress but did not know it. Sights, sounds, and smells would trigger it. I did not want to tell anybody what had happened because I thought they would think I was nuts and put me in a psych ward. I just kept everything bottled up and did not tell anybody until after I became a Christian.

SHAUN: With a story like yours, we find people will often be fixated on one specific minute detail from the afterlife encounter. When somebody reads your book or hears you share your testimony, what is that one thing you want every person to take away from your story?

BRYAN: Just realize that there is eternal recompense and you are not as good as you think you are. What was really exposed and what I want people to see is their pride. Pride is deadly. People are self-righteous and come up with all sorts of excuses for not following Jesus. All the while they are following the devil, controlled by addictions, drugs, or whatever, and their pride will not let them surrender. It is time to surrender yourself and say, "Lord Jesus, I do not want to go to the awful place. Take me. I am Yours." That is all I can ask.

The most important thing you need is Jesus Christ to save you, because He came and proved God's love. He showed you what God's love does in the Bible. People hate the Bible. Well, the Bible tells you to let us reason together. God reasons. Look at the world today. It is authoritarianism. It is cramming things down your throat against your will. That is not God. God reasons with you. He is good to you. He is always trying to woo you back, knocking on your door; and you do not want to come to Him because your pride is keeping you away. Look at the world. Do you want to live in this world of authoritarianism? Do you think living a debased lifestyle is a measure of God's love? How proud is that? Do you think that God's love is going to accept everybody into Heaven by osmosis and it is going to be great? That is you thinking that. That is your pride that must be surrendered. You must lay it down, and then after, as a Christian, when you are in your walk, you must be on guard against it, just like the apostle Paul was. You must always be on guard against your pride creeping up, against thinking that you are something when you are not. And that is the danger I see in a lot of people, which sends them straight to hell. When you have that revealed to you standing before the Lord, and you see what your stink and pride are like, how you justify yourself and all your acts, just listen to yourself sometimes in front of a mirror. My best takeaway is that you need Jesus Christ, who died on a cross to expose what we are really like to each other.

Jesus was betrayed. He was abandoned. He was plotted against. Everything you have done to everybody else, Jesus went through in the 24 hours before the cross, exposing what iniquity is like in us, how we make demands on people, how we want God to perform to our own liking—all that is displayed in that event. And then He was nailed to a cross, suspended between God and man, taking the wrath of God for us putting Him on the cross in the first place. A love like that is far too profound for me to wrap my head around. So God proved to me by the cross His great love, and the message I got out of this whole experience was a deeper appreciation and understanding of the cross and to convey that to people in the shortest amount of time possible so that they can just look up and say, "Lord Jesus, I do not want to go to the awful place. I know I am tired of living my life. I do not know how to change. Take me. I am Yours. I surrender." That is all I have. That is the most important thing that I ask people to do.

REFLECTIONS ON BRYAN MELVIN'S EXPERIENCE

RANDY: As with all of the afterlife survivors Shaun and I have interviewed, Bryan and I have become friends, but I can only relate to the vision of Heaven that God gave to Bryan after his hell experience. God gave Bryan a vision of Heaven after he suffered the effects of post-traumatic stress disorder (PTSD) following his horrific encounter in hell. Being in hell is worse than being in a war zone, I would imagine, because in war a person is not always being attacked, but in hell Bryan was constantly terrorized. Even though Bryan was a "militant atheist," Jesus had searched his heart to know that Bryan would eventually accept Christ as his Savior, so Jesus gave to Bryan the secret for preventing his being devoured by demons. Jesus Christ told Bryan to declare His name as protection against the evildoers, and that should encourage all of us that there is indeed power in the name of Jesus Christ!

Bryan detailed several deceased persons in hell, such as a nineteenth-century womanizing preacher, which informs us that just professing oneself as a Christian is not enough to avoid eternal damnation. One must be truly born again as Jesus stated in John 3:3. John 3:15 states that whoever believes in Jesus Christ will "have eternal life," so that preacher obviously never had eternal life. But one person Bryan saw in hell most certainly did not have eternal life: Adolph Hitler. Bryan recalled that Hitler repeatedly relived the horrors of the atrocities this despot committed in

STORIES OF HEAVEN AND THE AFTERLIFE

the world. One cannot help but feel the justification of Hitler's retribution in hell, but Bryan's story severely reminds us of the need to share the light of Jesus to those around us before it is too late. Hell is real. Many have a tough time reconciling a loving God with the existence of hell, but Bryan helps us understand that Jesus truly desires that no one goes to hell, but that no one can enter Heaven except those who are redeemed through the saving grace of Jesus Christ. Otherwise, Heaven would be made imperfect. Hell from Bryan's and others' accounts is a place apart from the God of Heaven, and nothing good happens apart from God, and only evil thrives in God's absence.

SHAUN: There are three things that really stuck out to me from Bryan's story.

First, I want to comment on Bryan giving us a concrete example of pride coming before a fall. Within hours of drinking contaminated water, Bryan knew he was sick, but rather than doing the sensible thing and immediately seeking medical attention, he decided to go his own way and try to take care of things on his own. Bad decisions can have real consequences, sometimes to the point of ushering us through the gates of hell.

Second, I believe it is worth highlighting that Bryan's story contains all of the classic markers I would expect in a textbook out-of-body experience. That brief time before somebody crosses the veil into the afterlife tends to be marked by a cessation of pain, initial confusion, a realization that you are dead, floating away from your body toward the ceiling, and finally moving toward a tunnel or a light. The consistency of these out-of-body experience accounts lends strong credibility to the idea that there is a conscious and very much aware spiritual part of our being that continues to exist after the functions of our physical body cease.

Last, we should not lose sight of the accounts Bryan shared of people being continually tortured in hell. The detailed descriptions he gave help us to paint a more vivid picture of the horrors behind the phrase "weeping and gnashing of teeth."

FIND OUT MORE

If you would like to encounter more of Bryan Melvin's story, we encourage you to pick up a copy of his book *A Land Unknown: Hell's Dominion* (Xulon Press, 2005). You can also connect with Bryan at AfterHoursMinistries.com.

CHAPTER 4

JEWISH TEEN IS CRUSHED IN HORSE-RIDING ACCIDENT AND ENCOUNTERS JESUS IN HEAVEN

MEET HEIDI BARR

At age 16, Heidi Barr experienced a freak accident when the horse she was riding stumbled off a hillside and crushed her underneath. Although she had been raised Jewish, Heidi found herself holding hands with Jesus.

In this conversation, Randy and Shaun talk with Heidi about her out-of-body experience in Heaven with Jesus, what happened when she returned to her body, and the ways her heavenly encounter has impacted her work as a hospice nurse, sharing the hope of Heaven with the dying and their loved ones.

INTERVIEW WITH HEIDI BARR

RANDY: For a near-death experiencer, Heidi Barr has a unique perspective from several vantage points. She has worked

105

as a hospice nurse, meaning she has spent time with many patients who are going through the death process. She had her own near-death experience at age 16. And last, she is a Jewish believer in Jesus.

Heidi, take us into the horseback-riding incident that resulted in your journey to Heaven.

HEIDI: When I was 16 years old, I was riding my horse bareback out at the ranch where we boarded her in Iowa where we lived. My sisters were there with me. My 14-year-old sister stayed in the car with the windows rolled up because she is allergic to horses.

After riding for about an hour I decided to go back to the barn because I figured my sisters were getting bored. I headed back to the barn and above the barn was what we called the Ridge Trail. It was a trail along a hill that overlooked the barn and the valley on the far side and in front of the barn. I rode to the end of the Ridge Trail, which was a dead end. The only way to get off the trail was to go back to the barn. I was sitting there enjoying the view when suddenly I heard hoofbeats behind me. I knew exactly who it was. It was a man on an out-of-control Arabian.

He was coming fast, so I just stayed on my horse because most horses when they are running out of control will run back to the barn. I assumed his horse would do that, but instead the horse with the man flapping wildly and crazily on his back came down the Ridge Trail.

I froze because I did not know what to do. I did not know if I should jump off my horse because I was afraid I would be trampled if there was an interaction between the two horses. I thought, *Okay, once this horse sees my horse standing calmly, he will stop.* But he did not. He ran right into my horse and my horse reared up. The first time she reared, I dropped the reins and just grabbed her neck. The second time she reared up, she stepped backward off the Ridge Tail and flipped over upside down onto me. We flipped off the trail and down the slope. She rolled across my body, and as she hit my chest, I knew I was dead. Every cell in my body stood stock still. I instantly left my body and was 30 to 40 feet up in the air. I saw my horse roll over my body and my body being tossed like a rag doll. I did not care. My body meant nothing to me. I knew it was me immediately, but I did not care.

I saw my horse slide down the slope, right herself, and head to the barn. My middle sister put her hands against the car window with a look of horror on her face. My little sister screamed and covered her face with her hands. I saw the man on the Arabian run. The Arabian turned and ran down the other trail toward the barn. I saw a lot of commotion in the barn, which was odd because the barn faced away from me, but I could see into the barn. The one thought in my head at that moment was that I wished my sisters did not have to see me die. I did not care that I was dead.

At that moment I noticed there was a light over my shoulder. As I had that thought, I saw that the light was illuminating everything before me, and suddenly I realized it wasn't a light but a man. The light was emanating from this man. He moved forward until He was beside me. I looked at Him and recognized Him immediately. It was as if I said, "Hi, how are You?" I knew Him. I had always known Him. I had known Him since I was a small child. It was Jesus, which did not strike me as being odd at all. At that moment, it should have been odd because my father was an atheist and my mother was an agnostic. Even though we were part of an Orthodox community, my father told us on an almost daily basis that Jesus Christ is the biggest hoax ever perpetrated on humanity, Christianity is a hoax, and Christians are stupid for having hope—all this because my father believed there was no Heaven, hell, or God. When you die, you are buried and forgotten. You are no more significant than the tiniest speck of dust in this infinite universe. So Jesus was the last person I should have encountered, yet He was the first person I encountered.

SHAUN: Heidi, I am curious to hear how you knew it was Jesus. Many of our friends who have shared about their near-death experiences say that in Heaven you are able to communicate without talking. It is more of a thought-to-thought sort of communication where you just know. You do not even have to try to communicate. When you encountered Jesus, did He say anything to you or is that simply what you were sensing in that first part of your journey?

HEIDI: Well, we immediately recognized each other. In fact, we were talking the entire time we were together. I cannot tell you everything we said now, because even though I was dead, I knew everything that was going on. And what I realized was that all of my questions were answered. You know, all of those existential questions, those nagging questions: Why am I here? What is the meaning of life? Is there a God? Is there a Heaven? It was all answered. I had no more questions and Jesus and I had all the time in the world, because time was immaterial. It simply was not a factor. When we communicated, did my lips move? I do not know if my lips moved, but we could still communicate. It was heart to heart. It was mind to mind.

We talked about my life. We discussed everything. And the thing is, I had known Him since I was a little girl. I had always believed in God, despite my parents, and I realized that He was the one I had been talking to my entire life when I prayed at night. And I would have conversations with God every night. That was Him. He had been by my bedside. And I always had a tangible feeling that He was there. So yes, we did talk how we talked. Did we say things aloud? I heard Him in my head, so maybe.

RANDY: Heidi, it sounds like you had believed in God and you had prayed to God, yet you had been told that Jesus Christ was a fake. What was it like to go from a point where you believed in God to realize you were face to face with Jesus Himself?

HEIDI: For me, it was recognizing an old friend. I had known Him since before I was born. I had always known Him and I recognized Him and had no difficulty recognizing Him. And as weird as it is to say this, it did not surprise me. It did not shock me. It was a reunion. Jesus and I had a joyous reunion. That is the best way I can describe it because I just turned to Him and He said, "I know you." Then He started to laugh. He didn't say, "I am Jesus; believe in Me." People often wonder if He came at me with fire and brimstone or if He announced Himself. No. I simply knew who He was. There was no doubt in my mind. It was Jesus and He had always been with me. He was my best friend, my Father, my Brother, everything. He was everything to me at that moment.

SHAUN: Next, Heidi, I would like to hear what it was like to cross from our world to the other side and what it was like to travel with Jesus.

HEIDI: The best way I can describe it is that it was like flying with Superman. He was such fun. We laughed the whole time. He took my hand and we left the barn area. I am going to be honest with you, I was so busy looking at His face that it was hard for me to attend to what was happening behind Him. So, what I saw passing was, as I looked at His face, I could see things passing behind Him. It seemed as if we were passing things on Earth. I could see individual things and we were surfing on a wave of light. I looked down and I could see both of our feet and underneath our bare feet was this rolling wave of light.

It was like body surfing on waves of light that were all colors. We kept going faster and faster. I saw that ahead there was a barrier. I cannot explain the barrier, but it was as if we crossed a threshold. Think of it as a door where you are stepping through a threshold or over a threshold. At that point I could not differentiate individual things. Everything seemed to become one thing and that one thing was God. I was still an individual and He was still an individual, but I saw that all of those things were God. And it was after we crossed this threshold that we came into a light.

SHAUN: Heidi, I would love to hear a bit more about your life review. Many of the people we have talked to previously had their afterlife experience when they were well into adulthood. You had this experience at age 16. What does that look like when a 16-year-old has a life review?

HEIDI: Well, I was a rather good kid. I was having some issues at that time. I had experienced a great deal of abuse in my 16 years. And at that point I was fighting back and rebelling. I was using drugs and hanging out with kids I should not have been. When I had my life review, Jesus did not focus on that. He did not give me any lectures or point an accusatory finger at me. He did not tell me to stop doing drugs and hanging out with those kids. What I received was a life review that was short because as I said, I was a good kid. I was nice to people, even if I was hurting myself. What He showed me was that I was judging myself.

Jesus was pointing things out. He was there saying, "Well, why don't we look at this? Why don't we consider this? What do you think about that?" But He was not judging me. I was judging me. And the one thing I saw and felt was, if I hurt someone, if my words hurt someone, I felt what they felt. I understood the impact my words and actions had on other people and it changed me. I am not perfect, believe me. I can cuss with the best of them and I can yell at my kids and my husband. I get mad. This changed me in that I am very aware of what I do. I am aware of how my actions impact others and I pay attention to myself. But as I said, my life review was short because the only person I was really hurting was me. The things I saw in my life review impacted me when I came back to life.

RANDY: Heidi, many people want to know what Jesus looks like physically. Can you give us a description of Jesus? Also, tell us if there was anything from your Jewish heritage that impacted how you understood your encounter with God in Heaven.

HEIDI: Well, I had a surprisingly good Orthodox education because our synagogue was Orthodox. Even though my parents did not believe, we went to synagogue and spent a lot of time there. Jesus is perfect. He is perfection. Randy, you have probably experienced this as well. His hair was about my length. It was a chestnut brown and had some streaks in it. It was wavy. He had a lean face with some scruff, you know, a beard and mustache, but not too long. He had a beautiful mouth, a gorgeous smile. I couldn't look away from His smile. It was infectious. His eyes radiated all the joy in the universe. This was hard for me to tell anyone at first, but His eyes are blue. They are the most beautiful blue eyes I have ever seen. I did not want to say anything about that because even though people in my family have hazel eyes, my father has green eyes. Most Jewish people I know have brown eyes, but Jesus had blue eyes. I thought nobody was going to believe me if I said Jesus had blue eyes.

In terms of build, he was between 5 foot 9 and 5 foot 11, slender, and around 160 pounds. He was wearing a white robe. His hands were slender and His fingers were long and tapered. He had beautiful nails. His feet were like mine, long slender feet, with long toes, which I thought was cool. The only thing I will say, which it may sound like an imperfection, but it was not: I really appreciated His nose because it was crooked. I thought, *Wow, He has a crooked nose. That is so great.* It gave His face so much character. He was the most real person I have ever met. His face was the most real face I have ever looked at in my life. So that is what He looks like.

SHAUN: Heidi, that is the most detailed description of Jesus that we have received in our series of NDE interviews. I find it intriguing that many of the people Randy and I have spoken with have told us that Jesus has blue eyes. You are one of several near-death experiencers who noted that specific feature of His appearance when they shared their story with us.

Thanks for taking a few moments to deviate from the timeline of your story to tell us what Jesus looked like. Pick up the story from where you left off. What other sorts of things did you encounter on the other side of the veil?

HEIDI: After we crossed that barrier, this light, the only way I can describe it is to say it was alive. How is it light can be alive?

JEWISH TEEN IS CRUSHED IN HORSE-RIDING ACCIDENT

It was love. It was a blemish-free white light. It was perfect. It filled my entire field of vision but did not hurt my eyes. It did not burn me. Jesus and I flew directly into the light. I knew that light was love, I knew it was living, and I knew it was God. Jesus took me straight to God and I sat on His lap. And at that point, Jesus vanished; He disappeared from my view and became part of the light. This part of my journey is difficult to explain, but I honestly could not see God's face.

As I said a moment ago, I found myself sitting on God's lap and my face was buried in His chest and my arms were around Him. His arms were around me. I was kicking my feet like a little kid and I never wanted to move. I did not look up at His face and I do not know if I would have been able to see it if I had tried, because it was surrounded by clouds. Sitting on God's lap was the most marvelous experience. It was beyond words. I felt loved. I felt that I belonged. I felt that I was home. I never wanted to leave Him. I would have sat there for all eternity, with my face buried in His chest, and I would never have moved.

RANDY: Heidi, all of our guests have said that they did not want to leave Heaven. Tell us what happened next in your conversation with the Lord that caused you to have to return to this world.

HEIDI: When I was sitting on God's lap, He and I did not speak. I just knew He was love. I do not know how a light can be a man and a light at the same time. I do not know how something can be the living embodiment of love. I have no clue how to explain it, but He was all of those things. As I sat there, I did not want to move my head; I just wanted to stay there. Next, He moved, shifted so that I had to lift my head. I could see that He had pulled away a corner of Himself, infinitely far away.

When He withdrew that corner of Himself, I could see what I can only describe as Heaven. And the first thing I saw was grass. It was this amazing green grass. This was infinitely far away, but I could see every single individual blade of grass and it was a brilliant green. The colors were beyond what we have here on Earth. The most beautiful colors here are merely a shadow by comparison. They are only a reflection of the colors in Heaven. I could also see flowers. I could see every petal of every flower and every vein in every petal of every flower and every pistil and stamen of every flower and every grain of pollen. I could see trees. I could see every leaf on every tree, every individual leaf, every vein on every leaf.

They were all moving, but there was no wind, but they were moving with the light and they were singing the praises of God. The grass was singing. That was the thing that just awed me— the grass. Every blade of grass was singing the praises of God.

And I could not look away. And then I saw, as I looked farther, that there was a meadow and I could see a misty pathway that was shrouded in clouds. It was as if there was a veil between that, what was coming down the pathway, and myself. I could see people were coming. I could hear singing, but I could not make anything out clearly. I just saw people were coming toward me on that pathway.

This was all far away, but I could see every detail. And it was at that moment, as I was staring at this, that Jesus came and stood right next to me. And He said, "You did not die. You must go back." I buried my face back in God's chest, and I said, "I am not going back." And He said in a clear voice, "You did not die. You must go back." His voice was clear as a bell. And I said, "No, I do not. I am not going back. I am not going back." He took my hand and I kept screaming at Him, "I am not going back. I am not going back. You cannot make me go back." I was having this huge argument with Him. And as He pulled me off God's lap, I remember screaming, "I will feel pain." And the next thing I knew, there was no surfing, no tunnel, nothing. Bam!

We were right above my body and I did not want to get in my body, but He shoved me in. I call it hoovering. I was hoovered in, vacuumed into my body from underneath and hit my face. Think about being shoved into a box and hitting the inside of the box. I hit the inside of my skull and I panicked. I had the worst panic attack you can imagine. I felt trapped in this body, but the next thing I knew Jesus was in my body with me. The only way I can describe it is to say that He smoothed my arms into my arms and He smoothed my legs into my legs. He made me one person again. And He said one last thing before He left me, which was, "Your life is in good hands." That was something that haunted me for years. It took me a while to remember how to open an eye, how to talk. I was gravely injured, but I did eventually manage to crack open an eye. I saw the ranch owner kneeling next to me, crying. I croaked out his name and the rest is history.

SHAUN: Wow! That is the most dramatic body re-entry story that we have heard thus far. So you are back in your body and are still injured from your horse rolling over you. What happened next?

HEIDI: Well, I was lying on my left side in a heap and Charlie threw me over the horse, which is the last thing you want to do to someone who just died. But he threw me over the horse and we went racing down to my car. He threw me in the back of my car, drove right past the hospital, and took me home. As I said, my family was a little odd, so he carried me upstairs, laid me on my bed, and I could not move. I had no feeling from the waist down. I had a fractured pelvis, broken back, crushed chest, and multiple other injuries. My parents left me there for 24 hours.

My mother put a heating pad on my back. And since I could not feel it, I ended up with a third-degree burn. When I still could not walk the next day, I crawled on my arms down to the car so I could get to a clinic. And he sent me straight to the hospital, but it was not a trauma center. There weren't any neurosurgeons or neurologists there. I was on my back for a month.

It was a difficult recovery, but the miracle is that I recovered. I made a full recovery without much intervention or therapy. The vertebra in my lower back fused themselves. I did not have anything done. This was truly a miracle recovery. I was out of school for a while, but I did start school in the fall on crutches. I was changed when I came back. I stopped doing drugs, stopped smoking. I broke it off with the kids I had been hanging out with. Jesus did not tell me to do that. I just did that. And I kept my head down, stopped rebelling, graduated from school a year early, and went to Israel, because if there was one thing I knew, it was that I needed to go to Israel to walk where Jesus had walked. I had to be there. I was Jewish and I wanted to go to Israel. I learned Hebrew, went everywhere I could, and walked where He had walked.

RANDY: There is something special about a Jewish person who finds their Messiah. It is like they have finally come home. Now, I had the benefit of spending some time with you during a filming and got to know you personally. I can tell everyone that you are on fire for the Lord. Heidi, when you returned from Israel, how did your family respond to your faith in Jesus Christ?

HEIDI: I still have a relationship with them. It is dysfunctional for other reasons, but on the second day I was hospitalized I did tell my parents that I had died, met Jesus, and gone to Heaven. My father went deadly silent and got pale. My mother just said, "Oh, don't be silly." They called in a psychiatrist. Next, they called in a rabbi who was an atheist. The psychiatrist did not talk much about this. He just talked around it. He listened to me, but he did not say anything, which was a good thing.

The rabbi just said, "Oh, we imagine a lot of things when we are unconscious." I told him, "I was not unconscious. I was dead." After that I didn't talk about it. My father has in fact never read my book because he does not want to deal with death and dying and he certainly does not want to deal with the fact that I died and met Jesus. We do not talk about it. My sisters and I have talked about it, especially my little sister. She was very impacted by this accident, so I can talk to her about it. My kids are aware of the story, but it was not until I heard John Burke interviewed several years ago that I contacted him and was able to talk about it. I cannot talk about it with Jewish people because "Jesus" is a bad word. I am Jewish, my kids are Jewish, and I am married to a Jewish man.

It was hard for me to open up to Christians as well. I thought people were not going to believe me. I know the experience was true—the truest thing that has ever happened to me, the most real thing. It was real real. The only way I can describe it is that it was real. And I just decided I am not going to talk about it. So it took me a lot of years to go public with this. It is difficult to be a Jewish person who met Jesus and accepts Jesus as the Jewish Messiah. It is hard. You do not really fit into the Jewish community anymore. So I am not a Jew for Jesus. I am not going to be in an airport telling people to believe in Jesus. That is not my thing.

SHAUN: Next, Heidi, I would love to hear about how your experience ties into your life and calling. People who come back from Heaven are profoundly marked by what they experienced. Did you see yourself as having a specific purpose or mission that God sent you back for? Was there a specific reason you became a hospice nurse?

HEIDI: You know, He did not give me any mission. What I learned was, you die, you go to Heaven, you meet God, you come back, you live your life, and you be a good person. That was the basic message I got. And what I knew was that I wanted to have children and raise them to be good people. I never intended to become a nurse. It was the last thing I wanted to do. My goal from the time I was a child was to be a great writer.

I majored in creative writing with a minor in religious studies, specializing in Judaic studies.

I ended up getting married to someone else, had a kid, and could not get a job after the divorce, so I went to nursing school. It was the most practical decision I have ever made and I do not tend to be a practical person. I loved it and intended to become a nurse midwife. That did not work out because I had to make money, so I went into coronary care and intensive care. That was where the money was. I had to support my son and I did that for a lot of years. And then one day I stepped into hospice. I was dealing with a lot of dying people in intensive care and in coronary care. I lost a lot of patients.

Basically, they either die or they live when they are in intensive care or in coronary care. There was one person who touched me and it shifted my focus from bringing life, helping to usher life into this world, to helping to usher life out of this world. I view it as two sides of the same coin. I do not view it as death. I view it as another birth. And I got a job working full time as a hospice intake coordinator, and then decided I would rather just see patients myself and did that for 12 years until we moved up here. It was great.

RANDY: Most people struggle with the idea of dying. There is nothing grandiose about the process itself. The body gives way and it succumbs; the heart stops, the brain follows, and that stops as well. How do you minister to or encourage somebody dying or the loved ones of somebody dying, knowing what you know about Heaven? Because, bottom line, we are all going to be there.

HEIDI: Dealing with the death of the patients I have taken care of was not easy for me. I have spent a lot of time crying with patients and crying with their families, but I am confident. They trust me because they can see my confidence that I am not afraid of death. I am afraid of getting old and infirm. Nobody wants that to happen, but I am not afraid of death. My patients and their families have noticed that. I hold hands. I am willing to listen to anything anyone has to say. I am willing to listen to any fears, any angers, any hurts, any slight. I do not judge. I am not going to judge. That is not my job. My job is to provide comfort and to ease suffering. And that is what made me a good hospice nurse. I have a great affinity, a great compassion for anyone who is suffering. If I can ease the pain, ease the suffering, ease the transition, God will handle the rest. I have every confidence in God's ability to take care of what He needs to do for every single person, every single soul on this earth. I do not have to control that. I am willing to turn that control over to Him.

The biggest thing I have learned is that I do not have to judge my patients. I have taken care of patients who were everything from drug dealers to mafia. It is not my job to judge them. It is my job to ease their pain. And I have gotten attached to most of my patients. Some were difficult, but even those patients I am not going judge. I am just going to deal with their issues. So I just have confidence in God that He is going to judge. If He took care of me, He believed me, then He is going to take care of them. If He took care of me with my background, then He is not going to abandon anyone. What we decide in this life and after this life is up to us. We still have the capacity to make our own decisions.

We have free will. God and I talked about that a lot when I was going through a difficult period after my divorce, the first time around. I realized that it is our decision. God opens a lot of doors for me and a lot of times I just run into the wall instead. That is what I do. I am very headstrong. He knows that. He knows everything about me. Sometimes when I do stupid stuff or I am stubborn, I am like He made me; He knows what I am. I am going to do a lot more stupid stuff in my life, but He gave me those choices. He did not say, you have to do this. He gave me a whole lot of choices. He gives us all choices

SHAUN: I think dealing with our own children helps us to understand how God is with us. He wants the best for us and gives us the guidance; but just like it happens with our own kids, sometimes we do run into that wall and make those interesting decisions. I find, more often than not, that we learn a lot in that process, on our journey with God, and as we are parenting our own kids, even into their adult years. Heidi, I want to make sure we have you mention your book. Tell us what people can expect there.

HEIDI: The title of my book is *One Foot in Heaven: Journey of a Hospice Nurse.* I wanted the stories to focus on my hospice patients, because it is their journeys that really changed my life for the better. I do touch briefly on my own near-death experience. When I was writing the book, the publisher made me take out any references to Jesus. I want to be clear about that. He wanted this book to be ecumenical and not put anyone off. He wanted everyone to read it. I have not rewritten it. I have left it alone. John Burke is bugging me to write a second book, which I will be doing. In the meantime, you can find *One Foot in Heaven* on Amazon. And as my little sister says, you will laugh, you will cry, you will be horrified, but you will love the book. There is a lot of interesting stuff that happens when you are a nurse.

RANDY: Heidi, you and I share that too, working in clinical settings. I was more on the business side, working within the operating room, and you were on the nursing side, working both in the intensive care and cardiac units and now with hospice. There is a difference I think for those who come from a clinical background having this experience than for those who do not, because I don't know about you, Heidi, but my propensity is to want to put it in terms of what is going on physiologically and psychologically. God turns that upside down with an experience in intimacy, as you said, the person within the person of love versus what our perception of love is. You and I share that because how do you describe love as a person and not just as an emotion?

HEIDI: The only thing you get to take with you when you die is love. You do not get to take anything else. There is not a single material thing on this planet that I could not lose. I could lose anything that I own, any possession. Those things do not matter to me. What matters are the people in my life. Sure, it is great to be comfortable. It is great to have a house. It is great to have a roof over my head, but if I lost all of that, I would still have God. The only thing you get to take with you is love, nothing else.

RANDY: Shaun, you have the vantage point of having heard many of these NDE stories. Do you see a continuity between those and what Heidi shared? What is your takeaway?

SHAUN: On the one hand, there are a lot of commonalities between these experiences, but it does seem that God gives each person an afterlife encounter that is tailor-made for them. What they experience on the other side of the veil tends to be specific to what they love and who they are at a deep level. God seems to respond and connect with each person in a way that is significant and meaningful for them. The part that really sticks out to me from Heidi's journey is spending time in God the Father's lap and just being able to hug Him. That must have been extremely significant for you, Heidi. As you have pondered and processed this through the years, what part of your Heaven journey stands out the most for you?

HEIDI: Sitting in God's lap was the best thing in the history of the world, since time was created. I thought surfing with Jesus was great, but that was the best. I do not think it would have mattered what age I was. When you are sitting on His lap, you are still a little kid in your father's arms. And like I said, I was kicking my feet like a three-year-old. There was just this sense of belonging and perfection and acceptance. It did not matter what I had done or had not done. He loved me exactly the way I was. I have an exceptionally good memory and can remember back a long way, but these memories are just burned into my consciousness. You do not forget this stuff and you do not forget the feelings associated with them.

When I met Randy, he was just a sentimental guy and tears up easily when he talks about his experience. I do not because all I remember is this amazing, incredible joy. This joy was beyond words. Having my kids was similar, but it was the most joyous thing that has ever happened to me.

RANDY: Heidi, I have one final question. You had a lot of difficulties in your childhood. Based on your experience in Heaven, what is your encouragement to somebody who has had to endure abuse and trauma during their childhood?

HEIDI: My life did not change immediately. I went through a lot more after that experience. But when I say that, the last thing Jesus said to me was "Your life is in good hands." That haunted me. I felt guilty because I felt, why me? Why isn't everyone's life in good hands? And then it hit me. Everyone's life *is* in good hands. Whether what happens is good, whether what happens is challenging, whether what happens is tragic or sad, He is still there. And the thing that always kept me going was the fact that I knew God was with me; whatever was happening with me, He was right there with me. And I will be very honest and say that I have never felt angry with God. I have never blamed God. I had this sense that whatever was happening to me was not happening because it was God's plan.

It was not happening because God was all in with this. It was happening because human beings are flawed and sinful. What I realized was that even if horrible things happened in my life,

God would still be with me. My life would still be in His hands. That is what I learned and it did not mean, here, I now give you a perfect life. That is not what it meant. None of us has a perfect life. And I am so sorry for everyone who experiences abuse. I feel fortunate because God created me an optimistic, cheerful person. I am a happy person. The abuse has affected my sisters differently than it affected me. And they have struggled. It might seem weird to say this, but dying gave me a new lease on life. My sisters have continued to struggle in their lives with what we experienced. It is just such a hard subject. If any of your readers are experiencing abuse, I understand, I am sorry, and I know God is with you. It may not seem like it, but if He was with me, then He is with you too.

REFLECTIONS ON HEIDI BARR'S EXPERIENCE

RANDY: I met Heidi during a dinner with John Burke, author of *Imagine Heaven*, and I was instantly impressed by the joy she experienced in having met her Jewish Messiah, Jesus, in Heaven. Two things struck me about Heidi. One, Heidi rediscovered her Jewish roots through a personal encounter with Jesus the Messiah. Before then Heidi really did not know much about Jesus since God was rarely talked about in her household. And two, she served as a hospice nurse who helped many people ease into their eternity during the dying process, and having died and met Jesus in the afterlife, she brings a true understanding of what lies on the other side of this life. I remain fascinated by how Jesus uniquely reveals Himself to others in Heaven. For example, Heidi faced abuse in her early years and ministered to the terminally ill vocationally, so Jesus took Heidi on a kind of "joy ride" through Heaven. Heidi describes it as a type of roller coaster of light, and Jesus laughed much of the way. I wonder now if Jesus had tailored His revelation to Heidi as a means of healing some of her past sorrows.

For me, I felt abandoned by God before dying and meeting Jesus. Knowing the condition of my heart, Jesus never let me go in Heaven. He hugged me tightly and I always felt as though I was the only one who mattered to Jesus. I think of John, who described himself as "the disciple whom Jesus loved." Obviously, John needed to feel special. When Heidi first shared her full afterlife story with Shaun and me, she chuckled a bit remembering how Jesus laughed with her. I gleaned a sense of joy emanating from Heidi as she shared her intimacy with Jesus in this way; and now having gotten to know Heidi, I can see that Heidi's greatest joy happens when she talks about Jesus and their kindredness. That special bond resulted after Heidi was crushed by her horse, and it strikes me as extraordinarily ironic that the most joyous day of one's life (entering Heaven) will most likely follow the most tragic event of a person's experiences: death. Jesus does truly redeem our sorrow with joy.

SHAUN: There are three things that really stuck out to me from Heidi's story.

First, I want to comment about the concerns she had during her out-of-body experience. Rather than solely having concern for her own dire circumstances, she was concerned about the trauma her sisters would endure from watching her die. This is another splendid example of how a person is conscious and aware after their spirit leaves their body, able to both think and feel emotions.

Second, I am fascinated that Heidi became a hospice nurse where she worked with people who were near death. It is hard to think of a better person to help them through that difficult period than somebody who has already been to Heaven.

Last, I want to make note of Heidi's experience of sitting on God the Father's lap. As Randy and I continue to encounter new NDE and afterlife stories, time after time the experience a person has with Jesus or God the Father seems to be individually tailored to what that person needs or how they can most comfortably receive from God. This one aspect is always extremely personal, like God knows each one of us thoroughly and completely.

FIND OUT MORE

If you would like to read more about Heidi's experiences as a hospice nurse working with people who are close to experiencing the afterlife, we encourage you to pick up a copy of her book *One Foot in Heaven: Journey of a Hospice Nurse* (independently published, 2013).

CHAPTER 5

MESSIANIC RABBI DIES AND ENCOUNTERS THE FIRE OF GOD'S GLORY IN HEAVEN'S THRONE ROOM

MEET FELIX HALPERN

Messianic Rabbi Felix Halpern died when his body became toxic after a medical misdiagnosis and the related wrong prescription.

In this conversation, Randy and Shaun talk with Felix about his out-of-body experience, the many things he saw in Heaven's throne room, and his encounters with demons in the second heaven. You are going to be amazed at the destiny-shifting revelations Felix brought back from his encounters on the other side of the veil.

INTERVIEW WITH FELIX HALPERN

RANDY: Our guest today is a messianic believer who came to know Jesus as Messiah. Rabbi Felix, it is an honor to speak with you. Take us into your backstory and then tell us how you came to have an afterlife experience.

FELIX: Thank you so much, Randy and Shaun. It is an honor to share what God is doing and certainly as a Jewish person who has come to know Yeshua as the Messiah. It is the most unexpected step that a Jewish person can imagine taking in their life. My father's side was raised Orthodox. My grandfather was an Orthodox rabbi and they were all killed in the Holocaust. My father was the only survivor and came to an understanding of some sense of Yeshua while he was in the Dutch underground. I was born in the Netherlands. Over the years, as I began to grow and have this yearning for greater and greater understanding, the Lord brought people into my life who began to lead me down this path, and I began to see things in a way that is completely opposite of what we have come to understand as Jewish people.

In the mid-seventies, I had a profound experience with Yeshua and became, as they say, born again. You truly do become born like a new creation and something changes inside of you, a true transformation. I began to appreciate the fact that

I had become fulfilled, completed as a Jew. It is not that you become somebody else; you do not become a Gentile Christian. However, you label it: I am a Jewish believer in Yeshua. And as you know, we have come to understand the importance of that. So that is how the Lord began to work in my life.

I started working in the diamond and gold business on 47th Street in New York City. The Lord kept me with the ultra-Orthodox and Hasidic communities for 25 years and the Lord blessed the work. I was vice president of a company, enjoying what I did, but I had come to the point where I loved the Lord so much more.

I had known the Lord for over 45 years, and this was the point in time when the Lord brought us through a sovereign revival in our life. I remember that He said at my office on 47th Street, "I am bringing you back to your people." And the Lord said, "I want you to liquidate your retirement. I want you to liquidate your savings accounts. I want you down to zero because I want to take you into a life of faith where you must learn, and I am going to lead you like I led Mosheh." My Hebrew name happens to be Mosheh. I did not make that immediate connection, but I had this encounter with God as a Jewish man. The Lord spoke through the Spirit of God, the *Ruach HaKodesh*, so profoundly, and this was the message I was bringing back to my Jewish wife from Brooklyn, who never even knew what a bill was.

We had built a house six months earlier and had a high mortgage payment. My daughter was half a dozen years away from college, and this was what I was going to bring home to share with my wife. Praise the Lord, she had already known what I was about to share with her. She said, "I know what you are going to tell me and we will trust God and take a step of faith." Within six months I resigned my position as vice president and off we went, taking this plunge of faith.

I share this testimony often and I tie it into faith because the adventure of faith is, one moment you are captain of the *Starship Enterprise*, going where you have never gone before, but the next moment you feel like you are the captain of the *Titanic*, where everything is coming down. Those quantum leaps of faith are the adventure with God, and I can tell you that ever since then the Lord supernaturally provided in ways that we would never have been able to factor into what this faith would cost us. The Lord was a miraculous hand of provision.

Then we started a messianic congregation that was birthed out of revival, where God was doing profound things in our lives for 20-some-odd years. Jewish people were coming in and getting saved and miracles were happening. This was in the time of the Pensacola and Toronto revivals and we were kind of just swept in. It was an extraordinary time. My wife, who was raised as a conservative Jewish girl, has always loved the

Lord and had profound experiences as a child; and God was speaking to her in dreams and visions. She was already at a place where God was going to use her life and how the Lord brought us together.

There was a time before we went into the messianic ministry when the Lord woke me up at 3:00 in the morning to His audible voice. And in my left ear, I could hear, "I am bringing you back to your people." That was a turning point for my life in terms of what we have done over the course of the last 25 years, but we never could have imagined what God would do with my life because of a doctor's error.

We take people to Israel every two years and had just come back from our June trip. On that trip, I had an amazing experience at the Wailing Wall. All the times I have gone to Israel and felt prompted to go pray and put my hand on the wall, nothing really happened. But this time, as I turned around to walk away, one of the messianic rabbis from Brazil, who was with us, said, "You need to go back. God wants you back there." I went back and put my hand on the wall and I just broke. I went down to my knees and felt the literal presence of Yeshua, Jesus, walking up from behind me, coming through the crowd of the hundreds of Orthodox, and putting His hand on my shoulder, pushing me down.

I went down prostrate at the wall and the Lord said to me, "Do not be discouraged. Do not grow critical of My people here. I love them and they will soon come to love Me, so do not grow weary in what I have called you to do. Do not grow critical, but begin to love them more than ever, because they do not even know that I walk amongst them here; they do not see Me. They do not know Me but know that I am coming soon."

That just arrested me, profoundly impacting me to such a degree that when I got home, I was no good to anybody. I could not get back to living. I was driving my wife, Bonnie, crazy. She asked me what was going on and I said, "Bonnie, I don't know. I feel that the Lord said that something is not done. It's not finished. I am supposed to go back." So I was sorting through what spiritual calling is and what this means emotionally. I go back to Israel anytime I am trying to discern. Three weeks later, I could not shake this yearning that was compelling me to go back for what I did not know. I said to Bonnie, "I only know this. I need to go back for seven days. Every morning I will go to the Wailing Wall and I will pray. That's it." And I said, "I am going to wait for God. I believe He's supposed to meet me where He spoke to me and that is why I am supposed to go back."

And for seven days, I did that every morning. And then in the afternoon, when I felt the unction of the Spirit that it was time to leave, I left and had amazing divine appointments and encounters. For example, we were able to pray over a Hasidic man who at first was not able to see more than an inch in front of his face. When we were done with our seven-day prophetic trip, I came back home and went in for my annual physical.

My health has always been good, but this time the doctor misdiagnosed me with a thyroid condition. She prescribed a medication incorrectly where I consumed seven and a half months' worth of medication in 29 days when I did not need it to begin with. Looking back, I can see that within three to four days, my body began to manifest what doctors call an inner storm. It was a tremendous amount of tension, pressure, and pain. My body felt like a furnace. I thought it was spiritual. Quite frankly, I thought it was part of the manifestation of my profound experience in Israel. I kept telling myself this was spiritual, that it couldn't be physical because I was healthy. This went on every single night for a month and half.

Everything was building up to one night in September. This was the most difficult night out of the entire month and I was feeling the symptoms of a cardiac arrest. You know: pain in the shoulder, pain in the arm, pain in the chest. Instead of telling my wife what was happening, I went downstairs at 3:00 a.m., thinking I was going to rest and believing that it would go away. Unfortunately, it did not. I got downstairs, laid down, and in short order my heart just stopped. And that was it. My soul jumped out of my body and my spirit began to rise in the room. My body was lying horizontally at that point, and from a height above, I was able to see my lifeless body on the couch.

I saw a bit into the future. I saw Bonnie and my children planning my funeral and I saw the grief and the sorrow on them. It was not even momentary. It was the only time something like that entered my being: that I was aware of this and a powerful angel. It felt like I was just brought into an emergency room and I was lying on an operating table and the doctors were working on me, but this angel was moving his hand over me. I had this sense that he was ministering to my soul. I did not know what that meant at that point in my life. It only had meaning 15 months later when I began to understand something. And in that place, I saw a white light, a cone-shaped cylindrical light up and to the right side of me, which I knew was Heaven. There was a brightness at the end of it.

And in no time, I was before the throne of God. When I share about the life and death aspect of it, it is hard for me to talk about it because I feel in that moment, the fragility of my physical life, the tearing between the mortal and the immortal. I feel like my chest can just collapse inside because I can relive that moment of when it happened and now understand what it really meant. So the Lord brought me into the heavenlies. I was before the throne and it was surrounded by a ring of impenetrable fire ripples, like ripples of fire that were inconceivable in terms of their depth. It could not be penetrated really. And I was on my face at that point.

SHAUN: Felix, you have an out-of-body experience, move toward a light, and now find yourself in Heaven's throne room. Were you actively thinking about the grandeur of what you were experiencing in Heaven or were you just so enraptured by the experience that you were just going through it?

FELIX: No, in that immediate moment I realized my circle of life had ended. I knew it when my soul began to step out of my body. There was an awareness and understanding in that split second.

SHAUN: Felix, you also mentioned that you encountered an angel who was ministering to you. Had you encountered angels before? Did you immediately realize that this angel was giving you triage?

FELIX: I had an encounter with an angel 25 to 30 years earlier when we went into revival and God was doing profound supernatural things among us. It does seem like angel encounters have become more common in this season. When I went to tape for Sid Roth's *It's Supernatural* last year, there was an angel in the car, angels in the studio, and an angel in the hotel room. In fact, it took me eight hours to drive nonstop from New Jersey to Charlotte. When I got there, if you had said to me, "Let's go to Miami," I would have said, "Okay, let's go." I had no fatigue. It was amazing! The Lord sent an angel to lift us up and carry us. It was the same way going back to New Jersey.

RANDY: Felix, I am absolutely enthralled with the throne of God and your experience before the throne. Let's pick up where you left off. You are prostrate before God. Tell us what else you saw and experienced.

FELIX: One of the lingering effects is that when I worship in the presence, I have to cover my eyes when I think about it because of the brightness. I share in my book, *A Rabbi's Journey to Heaven*, that I was incapable of handling the brightness of the glory of the fire of God and God's presence. In my opinion it was because I was not meant to stay there. For the redeemed who are staying there, it is different. However, my eyes were not able to absorb the fullness of the fire. My eyes felt heat and I was down prostrate before the Lord. My mind had no other thoughts. The only thing I could think about was that I was in the presence of God Himself, in the presence of the glory.

RANDY: Felix, one of the pleasures I have experienced in getting to know you is that you and I have some similarities between our Heaven experiences. You experienced the awe of God, being in the presence of the glory, and that glory transcended into your return as well. You became a changed person because of that. It was as though the glory of God was so effusive and so brilliant that you experienced that as a messianic believer in a way that was like you knew you were home. You found the Messiah and were in the presence of the glory of God and were changed forever. How did this impact your life and ministry after you came back?

FELIX: Randy, you touched on something that is a distinction from my former life. I have always had a love for people. That is why I started serving the Lord. I love people, have a heart for the lost, and want to see people healed. However, the love that I returned with from Heaven is on an entirely different level. It is the love of God. It is a love that when I see someone, I could weep. I had love for people and ministered in that regard, but now I flow in a love that completely enraptures my soul in a way that I must touch them, because it is not me but God touching people through me. That supernatural love has had a profound effect on both my ministry and my personal life. I do not think you could come back from Heaven without it.

I do not know how you can come back from Heaven unchanged. The Lord gave me a choice. He said, "This will be transformational or it will be transactional. And if it is transformational, it is going to come at a price." Transactional, I knew that meant that this would eventually wear off. I told the Lord I was willing to pay the price because I was not about to go back and lose what He did. The reality in our lives is that anyone who goes through this, the enormity of Him giving you your life back never leaves you.

In the six months following my near-death experience, I went through numerous tests to check for damage to my liver, kidneys, and other organs. My doctor said to me, "I have no explanation other than your blood work looks like a young stag." At the time of this interview, I am 69 years old and have many years ahead of me. To see the Lord transform you and give you your life back, for me that is a complete shift for the rest of my days. I believe that is why my experience resonates with so many people. Randy and Shaun, what you are doing through these interviews, it resonates with people because they are looking for truth. People are looking for hope. They are looking for something supernatural. They are coming out of a dark period. It feels like people are coming out of a dark forest and the light is breaking through for the first time in their disillusion and they are trying to put life back together again.

SHAUN: Felix, I could not agree with you more. Our interviews have been viewed across the globe and have impacted millions of people. The one thing that comes through repeatedly is that people are desperate for the hope of Heaven. I initially looked at these interviews as a publishing guy and focused on making an impact by hitting the highlights of each story. But God has been showing me that it is important to get these stories out simply to connect people to that hope of Heaven. He wants them to have a confidence that there is something on the other side for them when they cross the veil.

Felix, I also love how much your story parallels with Randy's. Both of you gentlemen are so marked by the love of God. It is not that you did not love people before; it is that the depth of the love you carry has shifted on this latter side of your journey. That is a great connection point between the two of you.

Next, I want to get back to the fire that you saw around the throne, especially since you have had more time to process this experience since you wrote your book. Was the fire a representation of the glory of God and was there a refining element of being in the presence of that fire? Please share any additional insights you have on the fire.

FELIX: I think it was the absolute purity, glory, and the nature of who God is. I did not interpret it as a refining fire in Heaven. Everything there is refined and perfect. Everything is in the state of the way He created it and has never changed. I do not even know if there is an adequate word in the English language to properly express how much it was beyond perfection. I believe that it is the fire, the purity, the heat, the absolute refinement of what refinement is. For example, in my years in the gold business, I worked for many years in a gold refinery, so I know how to refine gold. I have handled gold bars coming in, melted them down, and understand how it comes to its perfect purity and so forth. So I understand that aspect of refinement, but the refining fire and the gold, if you will, of Heaven are beyond purity, of whatever we think it is—it's beyond 99.9 percent. The reverential fear that is around is so profoundly deep and beyond what we could comprehend that we could not handle it in the natural world.

RANDY: Felix, you have been talking about the transformational versus the transactional. You shared earlier that God asked you to give up all of the wealth you had acquired by your work in the gold and diamond business and to follow Him. So not only were you transformed in terms of your love for others, but also He was requiring something of you to move forward in your ministry and service to Him. Tell us about that.

FELIX: I remember a Friday night in a worship service where I felt the tug of the Spirit of God calling us into service. I just could not find the path to get to where I would be serving the Lord in full-time ministry. Serving the Lord seemed like climbing Mount Everest. Every time I felt something advancing, I would find myself slipping down the mountain again, not getting traction to move forward. Then one Friday night, the Lord said to me, not audibly, but by a clear conviction of the Spirit spoken into my inner self, "I cannot give you what you want because your job has become your security. Your security has become your work, your income." That was when I knew I needed to resign my position. For context, this was in the early eighties and I was making $140,000-plus. In 1982, 1983, that was a lot of money. The Lord was saying that I needed to leave and resign my position. That is precisely what we did six months later, taking our step of faith into our Abraham journey.

Solomon says, there is nothing better than for a man to enjoy the fruit of his labor. There is nothing wrong with that. It is a matter of what we love more. The Lord used our life to impact a lot of businesspeople in our congregation who came in when they heard the testimony of what we did. I did not lose my job. We did not lose our home. We walked away from these things for God. That is not to say that is what people are supposed to do, but that is what the Lord had us do because of the sphere of influence that we would bring to Jewish people who very much can serve the spirit of mammon. We live and labor in a very materialistic area in the Northeast and that has been used by the Lord to bring a sense of new fire and revival to people to show them that it is okay to love what you do.

You can prosper, but the key is loving Him above all. I believe that is one of the things the Lord used our life to put on display, and the Lord has been faithful. Similarly, He said, "This could be transformational or transactional." I felt it was the same choice. When we went into revival, our life was turned upside down by the glory of God. We had so many manifestations and miracles, but I think that anybody who has an experience with God of any supernatural substance, like what we are speaking about, there is always the choice of transformational or transactional. I think that is always the case. I have seen so many people go through revival and then go back to where they started.

I believe that the Lord, through a doctor's error, gave me my life back, but He could have said, "No, I am not giving you your life back." Then I would not be here. But I believe that there is an assignment that comes to us. It is part of the call, part of the responsibility. Now I live differently. I eat differently. I live slower. I live life more as an observer. And I will also say, and I do not mind saying it because I write about it, that it has taken some time for my children and my wife to adjust to it because I am a different person. So I am adjusting with measured steps and learning how to balance it all. When He brought me back, I like to say He did not put me back together the same way. He gave me some keys that are the absolute assignment of my life. I am more connected now to my spiritual being than ever before. Sometimes I can still see from above certain things. I do not know, Randy, if you have had that experience, but you know, the body, soul and spirit for me, there is daylight between the three. I live each day with a realistic, tangible awareness of the three.

And in my first three days back, the Lord said, "I am going to put you in two books." Ezekiel and Psalms have to do with the calling of God to the Jewish people. I was in those two books for two years. Who does that? I mean, of the 66 books of the Bible, I was in two, and the Lord says, "I am going to put you in the book of Psalms and you are going to eat from that book." And then the Lord opened understanding that the book of Psalms is truly the handbook of the soul. If anybody wants to know about the relationship between the soul and the spirit, it is only in the book of Psalms, over 50 verses. *Oh, my soul, why are you downcast?* It is like the second person, right? Randy, why are you so troubled? The psalmist speaks to his soul that way. *Oh, my soul, come and worship the Lord.* And it begins to unfold. The important relationship that we have in the spirit governing the soul is that the soul constantly comes into submission. But it is beyond that too. The book of Psalms is the handbook of God's glory. There we learn how to give magnification and enlargement to Him.

RANDY: Most of the guests on our show have had some sort of an afterlife experience. Mine was almost 15 years ago and Felix's experience is still very fresh in his mind. Shaun, how do you interpret that from your vantage point, in terms of Felix's experience coinciding with the other stories that we have heard? Obviously, we are speaking to somebody who has been Jewish, is Jewish currently, and is a messianic Jew, and somebody who experienced God on those terms, which are also unique to our stories.

SHAUN: There really is something special about being able to connect with people who are still very near to their near-death experience. Looking back on all of our guests so far, we have had several who are between one and three years out from their experience. In the retelling of the encounter, there is a rawness and a newness of somebody who is actively still in that process of understanding and processing what they saw in Heaven. This is different from our friend Ian McCormick who had his experience in the late seventies. He has been telling his testimony and processing his experience for over 40 years.

To me it feels like there is a definite difference between somebody who had their experience recently and somebody who has been commenting about it for many years. Randy, I do not want to lose this thought, because Felix mentioned that the envelope always remains a bit open. I would describe it as the veil always being partly pulled back. I am curious, Randy; in your experience have you also had a foot in both worlds like what Felix described?

RANDY: Yes. Even though our lives have been quite different, I feel a kinship with Felix, like he is my proverbial brother from another mother. What is incredible to me is that because of our experiences in the presence and glory of God, there was a transference of that glory power that is truly transformational. I love how you used the word "transformational," Felix, because when I left my experience of dying and coming back, I was still in the corporate world and had a vastly different mission. I was reticent to move into the world of ministry, as God had not yet called me to even tell my story.

And we have talked about this, Felix, in terms of telling the story, because there are certain parts of Heaven that defy explanation; there just are not terms that are adequate to describe it. And yet, you know, we share our experiences to help people draw closer to God through confirmation of their belief. And there is almost a supernatural drawing in from people hearing these stories, because they see that this is real. What surprised me in the process is that even believers have this shadow of doubt that this may not actually be real. You see people transition where they will go through a death process, where they are struggling and striving and fearful, and others who are at peace and their transition is amazingly easy and comforting.

So back to your feelings on this because your experience now is just on fire. I mean, you are sharing the love of God. You are looking at things in a much more appreciative way. The book of Psalms has fed your soul. Your spirit is in constant communion with the Lord. And you have this vantage point that is unique because you have this confirmation of faith having witnessed the Lord God. How does that translate into your life from when you returned initially, when you woke up? I would like to get to the moment when you came back to this world; there is a stark contrast. Was there any remorse? What was your initial reaction when you went from that point of being in the throne room to being back in your body?

FELIX: There was a period of time when I didn't feel that I was ever fully back in my body. But first I want to touch on what you were just saying and then come back to that. The separation that I feel, a detachment from the mortal realm that I carry with me—there's always a sense of immortality on my shoulders, if you will. The experience of the freedom when the soul is set free must be like what a bird feels when it leaves the nest for the first time, feeling the wind under its wings for the first time. That freedom, that sense has never left me. And there are times when, to be frank about it, I say, "Lord, I cannot do this anymore because You are detached."

There is a learning how to live with that. And at the same time, I do not want it to change, not for the sake of the experience;

no, I do not want it to change, because I want to live in the state, when even Jesus said, that we are in this world but we are not of it. There is such an amazing peace and presence of God. And when I came back, in those moments I saw my wife's face and I saw what would be. It has taken her this long to forgive me for not calling 911. I just did not think about. I just did not make the connection. I ignored all the signs. I do not know how you feel, Randy, but sometimes I feel like I am an ant on the earth. I take my morning walks. I write about this, and I enjoy God and everything He does, but I can feel like I am one man on the entire planet.

RANDY: Shaun, this is how a lot of us feel. We feel disconnected from this world, like we are truly foreigners here. I have yet to meet a near-death experiencer who wanted to leave paradise and the presence of the Lord to return this broken world.

SHAUN: You are strangers in a strange land, profoundly feeling how much we are not of this world because we were created for Heaven. We were created to be in God's presence, and because you have experienced the fullness of that, I would imagine it feels like there is a part of you missing back here on Earth.

FELIX: There is such a thing as a quality separation, and had I left, it would have been a partial separation. There is a point in time when the Lord calls us home. The Lord does not want many people living the way they do. They cannot wait for the rapture. They cannot wait to go home to be with the Lord. Yeshua said that He has chosen to keep us in this world. And I believe that every single person has an appointment, a destiny, a calling to fulfill, and God does not want us leaving prematurely. I do not believe it gives God pleasure that people sit and cannot wait to be in Heaven, because they are missing something in the here and now; they are missing the fullness of the life in the here and now that God has given us. And I realize that when I leave again, it will be a full separation, a quality separation where I have fulfilled my mission and my purpose. I came back with such an appreciation for life. I do not want to go back because I am not done. Now that is why I love life now. I love that He gave me my life back and showed me that I must live and accomplish what He has called me to do. Jesus died for that.

RANDY: That is a striking contrast to selfishly wanting to be in paradise versus knowing that we have a calling and a purpose that need to be fulfilled. To end it prematurely would be to deny God that pleasure of us fulfilling our unique purpose.

Shaun, in terms of these afterlife or near-death experiences, how do you think those give us a sense of urgency to fulfill our purpose? But also for those who do not yet know Jesus as their Messiah, there is an urgency for them to come to know Him. There is no promise of tomorrow.

SHAUN: Randy, you and I have talked about this in previous episodes where so many near-death experiencers describe being fully immersed in God's love. Both of you gentlemen have talked about coming back dramatically changed in terms of empathy, love, and how you feel about others. My sense after all the conversations we have had is that because you have been so saturated to overflowing, there is an aspect of God's heart for the people that He has called you to reach that somehow manifests in that way. I do not know any other way to describe it. So, Randy, Felix, do you have more commentary on that in terms of this side of your journey, in terms of your burden, your assignment? How does what you perceive as God's heart play into that?

FELIX: I refer to this as "the gift" in my book *A Rabbi's Journey to Heaven*, because it is a gift that was given to me. And I asked the Lord, "Is this only for me because I went to Heaven and had this experience, or is this transferable?" Randy and I both know that what we went through is not transferrable, but our life and lessons and who we are today are transferrable and can help imprint people for greater glory for the Lord. Remember when the Lord told me I would be in the book of Psalms for 30 days? Well, 30 days turned into 60 days and 90 days turned out to be 18 months. When I came back, I could no longer accept the world of typical Christian church culture as it was when I left. I just could not see myself going back into certain things.

One of them was prayer. The Lord revealed the difference between transformational prayer and transactional prayer that is changing people's lives. And the only reason I talk about this is because I am back. I was given my life back to talk about it. Otherwise, I would not even know about it. And the Heaven soul cleanse that comes in the book that people are going through now turns convention on its head. Because if we think about it, let's say that 80 percent of our prayer life is consumed with transacting something with God, right? We are asking God to heal, to bless, to move, to touch our ministries, et cetera. It is always asking God for something; that in itself is not wrong. Yet what I am about to say relates to that other 20 percent of our prayer life that is in what I call the transformational space.

Transactional prayer has and is always dominated by I, me, and mine. Transformational prayer is always dominated by the Father, by talking about the Lord God. I began to realize that transactional prayer is a needs-based prayer life because we live on a needs-based planet. Heaven is easy, but Earth is hard. I have known the Lord for 45 years. I do not think I have ever been without an area that I did not need prayer for. And I think as long as I stay here, I will always have areas of prayer that I need. One prayer is answered today and a new one comes up tomorrow. You can pray for your children, your grandchildren, your wife, your family, your health, and on and on. It keeps going and never stops.

A cycle of needs-based prayer reproduces. It can breed a needy spirit, which I believe hinders the abundant life. The Lord showed me that transformational prayer is rooted in sufficiency. It is a sufficiency mindset. Transactional prayer that is needs-based is an insufficiency mindset. We are always needy. The Lord showed me when I went on this 30-day soul cleanse that we can reboot our system. For those 30 days we begin to starve our soul of the natural order of needs and give all of our needs to the Lord: *Father, I give You my needs for 30 days.* In those 30 days, every morning do the psalms that we have put together. Do no praying. Other than that, it is like a liver cleanse or any other cleanse of the body where you abstain from something to recharge the organs. I do not believe my results have anything to do with my Heaven experience. My soul and my brain are imprinted with the glory of God, the majesty of God, the things of God's nature. His handprint is everywhere.

I look up into the morning sky and I appreciate the majesty of His creation. Even as we speak, in my subconscious I am in a new operating system, my whole subconscious, my whole consciousness is completely transformed. And what that does is, it gets the ceiling feeling out of people's lives and puts them under an open sky. I can close my eyes and Heaven is right here. It is not way up there. It is here. When the Lord gave this, I said that this is one of the most important antidotes to the problems in people's lives. Living in a state of fear and living in a state of need are normal parts of church culture. If we go to a meeting with other pastors, we will sing a couple of sings, but the rest of the meeting is all about praying for the needs of the church and the needs of the people.

Imagine if this took place in a person's life. Let's reverse the formula so that 80 percent of one's life in now in the transformational space, the glory space, and the other 20 percent is in the needs-based space. Imagine the effect on your soul. It will reboot a person and put them in a new operating system, what I call a heavenly operating system. The Lord assured me that people can live in the atmosphere of God's glory, get rid of the ceiling feeling, and live what it means to live in the life of abundance. The only reason that we have never heard about it is that it has never been taught to us. I had to die and come back to receive it.

SHAUN: Felix, as a former tech guy, I love the operating system language. It is time to get your upgrade!

FELIX: Yes, get the upgrade before it is too late.

SHAUN: Felix, your examples of moving from transactional to transformational have been extremely helpful. What you are describing shows a difference in the depth of relationship. If I am always asking somebody for something, it seems like it is at a lower level. If I move into what you are calling us to, that is going to lead to a higher level of relationship and move us closer to God's presence. In His presence, all those needs that we worry about and are constantly praying about will be met. They are just taken care of.

Felix, in terms of your expertise and what you did professionally, you have experience with precious metals and gemstones. I would love some insight on how that experience informed and impacted what you saw in Heaven. We have had many people describe seeing gold, gems, and other precious things, but since that was your area of expertise here in this world, I would love to find out how what you saw and experienced in Heaven exceeded what you saw here previously in the natural.

FELIX: I was by a large river whose water was as clear if not clearer than crystal. I saw that everything God created had life. Everything had living quality to it and it was sustained entirely by the glory of God, right in His environment. Under the water in the river beds, there were diamonds, rubies, and other precious stones and semiprecious stones. I have handled millions of dollars worth of diamonds, but nothing compared to the brilliance and clarity of those gems in the river bed. Now I did not go down and pick up a diamond, but it was obvious to me that there was a quality about these stones that is unsurpassed in this earth, in this mortal realm. The most flawless diamond cannot compare to what I believe I saw because of my experience at the river bed, because everything was adorned with gemstones of perfection. It is God's design. It is His creativity.

SHAUN: Felix, thank you for that. I will get in my one last question and then turn it over to Randy to bring us on home. One of the things I wrote down in my notes is that you had mentioned seeing demonic hordes in the second heaven and we have never had a guest reference that before, so I would like to hear about that and understand the insight you received from what you saw and how you processed that.

FELIX: In the period of time—and it has not closed completely—that followed my return, the envelope was, I can only say, pretty wide open. Sid Roth put it this way: "It's like living in an eggshell, cracked with a light, always coming in from the other side." That is a better picture of it all.

The Lord invited me to see the second heaven where the demons were. When I was standing above the second heaven, I could see a clear separation, not like a firmament between Heaven and Earth, but there was a definite separation that I was standing on. There was a particular demon, and there were many in there, but this one demon tried to climb up and grab hold of my ankle, but it could not. It was pitiful. I can have pity on them because I realize that we go from glory to glory in Yeshua; we go from beauty to beauty. Who we are is always coming to a greater reflection of the glory of God, the majesty of Yeshua. But they are going from decay to decay.

They were horrible and pitiful looking in that they did not even know that they had no authority to come to me. They had no ability to grab hold of my ankle, and the Lord showed me why: because I am covered by the blood of Yeshua. I came back with an understanding of the kind of authority that we live in daily. It is both a passive and an aggressive authority. It is aggressive in that we can use it against the kingdom of darkness, but it is also passive in nature. We live in a constant state of victory and power to such a degree that from our feet, the ground on which we walk and all the way up to the heavens, those airways, we have complete authority. For that reason, I can raise my hand to the Lord to worship Him and the worship and everything that is innocent, the spirit, extend all the way up into the heavens. We have complete authority by the blood of Yeshua.

What we have done in the church world is replace soul problems with devil problems. Catch that for a minute. People have fewer problems with the devil than they realize. What they really have are soul issues. We have upset something that is great for the enemy. We have inadvertently given him authority or have let him think that he has authority that he just does not have. And of course I can do a teaching on this in the Scriptures to back this up. There is no demonic attack and no demonic principality that can come against the blood of Yeshua—just like the blood that protected the Israelites from the angel of death coming through Egypt, just like the 144,000 are sealed by the Holy Spirit. The blood of Yeshua is profoundly authoritative and powerful over every demonic principality, over every sickness and disease, and I think that we have lost the reality of the power of the blood of Yeshua.

Now that is a tough topic for Jewish people to understand, because the Jewish people are 2,000 years away from sacrifice and the shedding of blood, and it has become a Christian term and a Christian concept, but it is a very Jewish concept obviously—through the shed blood of the lamb, through the blood on the lintel posts, on and on. And part of Leviticus is about atoning and shedding blood. I think back to your question: that was transformative to such a degree that everywhere I go, I wear python boots when I minister. My python boots are an immediate lesson that the devil, the serpent, has been cast to the ground. He is under my feet and that is where he is going to stay.

RANDY: Felix is talking about how we will live in Heaven. We will live in Heaven in a constant state of worship, consumed with thoughts of Yeshua. We will be consumed by His ways because the spirit is dominant over the soul and we have a new spirit body. We will no longer be distracted by the things of the world. We will be engulfed and immersed in the presence of God almighty.

What you write about in your book, Felix, and what you are talking about is how we can take Heaven and the model in Heaven, which is perfection, and transfer that to the way that we live in this world: to be focused on God and the things of God, to give Him thanks, to recognize His glory and His presence and His creation in this world— thereby inviting the presence of the Lord to take dominance over us and the problems of this world we are consumed by. So if Heaven is the model, how should we live in this world?

This is a profoundly serious moment in our conversation, maybe even the most important part of this interview. Felix, we are going to hand it back to you to invite people to know Yeshua as their Lord and Savior.

FELIX: It is no time to die unless someone is ready to die. And there are things that need to be set right in people's lives to make them ready. I do not believe the premature death of an individual is God's method of choice. The method of choice is that our people, Jewish people, come to faith in Yeshua the Messiah. And so, Father, in Your mighty name, we pray to You, Lord, the God of Abraham, Isaac, and Jacob. Father, there is no one like You. There are no gods greater than You. There are no beliefs that are truer than Yours. There is no hope that is greater than Yours within the sound of our voices.

Father, there are those who may be in a hospital room right now. They may be near death, at a point in their lives when the doctors have given them no hope. I ask, Father, that You would reach into that person's hospital room and heal their body and eradicate that sickness, that cancer, that injury. I pray, Father, for that person who is dying of diabetes. They are at the end. There are no organs. There is no hope. There is nothing left for them. Raise them up. I pray, Father, in the name of Jesus. I pray, Father, that through the words of this interview You ensure Jesus is carried with a message of hope, life, and strength. He is the way and the only way that every one of us, Father, must come to that determination in our life. Every Jewish person must come to that determination in their life.

And so must you come to that determination in your life. The question is, are you at the end?

I learned and saw firsthand what happens when a soul leaves the body. It either rises to Heaven and the glory of God or it crash-lands in hell. It sounds harsh. It sounds terrible. It sounds horrific. It sounds hopeless, but it is because the decision that needs to be made must be made on this side. There is no other chance to make that decision. On the other side, regardless of what someone may tell you, or regardless of what some say, the body, the soul just floats, or it goes away or it disappears. No, it does not go away. It lives on. It either lives in eternal darkness where one continues to live each day in decay, like I saw, or one lives in eternal glory, majesty, joy, and life. There is a choice to be made. And if you are one who has not made the choice, it is no time to die.

The choice must be made now. The Bible says it is the time of your visitation. Now is the time of your salvation. Now is the time to, right where you are, put your hand upon your heart, Jew or Gentile, in the quietness and in the sanctity of your heart, and say, "I am sure of Jesus. Heal me. Come into my life that I may be a child of God, that You would cause me to be born from above, that You would show me, a Jewish person, Yeshua, my Messiah."

You may be a prominent rabbi. You may be a prominent rabbi in Jerusalem and are reading this and no one is around. And I am saying to you, grab hold of the truth of your Messiah that you already know has been stirred in you. Now is the time and today is the day. And in this moment, I ask, Father, that You, Lord, would visit all those who are reaching for You right now. They are calling to You right now. They are in their hospital room. There is a cancer patient. There is someone, Father, who got into a serious accident and may be in a coma and there is no hope. I pray, Father, that You awaken them and visit them. We give You glory and honor, Father, for all that You do and for all that You are, for everything, Father, the majesty and the perfection. And I thank You, Lord, for sending Your Son to die for us, that You loved us so much that You gave Your only begotten Son that we would have life and that we would have it abundantly, that Yeshua was the Passover Lamb who gave His life for us. In Jesus's name we pray. Amen.

REFLECTIONS ON FELIX HALPERN'S EXPERIENCE

RANDY: I love how Felix as a rabbi speaks of his Messiah in terms of the orthodoxy of Judaism. He cites rabbinical traditions and Christian theology within the same context. But despite being a trained theologian, when we asked Felix to describe how he was affected by Heaven, his tone changed. He now relates his time with Jesus not from a trained perspective; rather, Felix's takeaway is almost childlike. He describes life after Heaven in this way: "I take time to ponder the things of God, to dwell on God's magnificent creations." So now Rabbi Felix stops to smell the flowers. He dotes on his family members. Felix explains that he now sees God's signature in everything that is good. Heaven transformed Felix from a theologian to an appreciator of life born through the Creator.

When we hosted the first Christian afterlife conference (Afterlife 2022), Felix was invited to pray for people. His prayers were anointed with healing and he exhibited a tenderness of heart toward those experiencing suffering. When Felix and I spoke about our common experiences, I asked him if he saw people in the same way after Heaven. "No," Felix replied, "I see them more like Jesus sees them." I agreed. Heaven speaks of its Creator, because everything in Heaven was first spoken into being by God, and its perfection has never changed. Thus, once having visited Heaven, one cannot help but be transformed forever. That lingering effect of Heaven caused Felix to appreciate the small things because God is in the details. His signature can be found within the veins of a green leaf as profoundly as it can be found in the galaxies created by God. Felix transitioned from a diamond executive to a rabbi and finally to a messianic Jew in love with Jesus the Messiah.

SHAUN: There are three things that really stuck out to me from Felix's story.

First, I want to point out what I thought was significant from Felix's encounter with demons in the second heaven. As he recounted earlier, the demons had no ability to grab hold of his ankle or harm him in any way because he was covered by the blood of Yeshua. If you are a follower of Jesus, you are too! That same level of authority and protection is available to you right now here on the earth.

Second, Felix spent many years handling gold and precious stones during his years in the jewelry industry. I especially appreciated hearing his description of the precious stones he saw in Heaven, given that was one of his areas of expertise here on Earth.

Last, take note of what Felix talked about relating to not settling for a transactional relationship with God. Moving things up to a truly transformational level of relationship will come at a cost, a dying to self. Even though that may be the more difficult path, it is the level of relationship we have always longed to have with God. I encourage you to pursue this transformational relationship with reckless abandon. Do not miss this!

FIND OUT MORE

If you would like to encounter more of Rabbi Felix Halpern's story, we encourage you to pick up a copy of his book *A Rabbi's Journey to Heaven: A Miraculous Story of One Man's Journey to Heaven and Your 30-Day Glory Transformation* (It's Supernatural Press, 2021). You can also connect with Felix at chofesh.org.

AFTERWORD

WHY DO THESE NEAR-DEATH
EXPERIENCE STORIES MATTER FOR ME?

The plain fact is that each of us will cease from living in this world. Your odds of dying increase every year throughout life until the odds become a reality. The most certain possibility of a life is the end of life as we know it on this earth. Indeed, our physiological makeup undergoes a process of demise after we reach a relatively young age, meaning that most of us are in the process of physically dying, and yet a form of ourselves persists beyond any physiological endpoint. Death does not represent the end of life.

At any point in our life the physical components of our bodies will relinquish themselves to a reality far exceeding the lifespan of this one. The works that we have produced will live long after their maker, which can be represented as our effect on others in the world to the everlasting imprints that will soon make their marks in the netherworld. There is a spiritual dimension that survives our physiological expiration, which will ultimately be decided by God—forever. In dying, we enter our unknown to that which is known by God.

True existence may be less about defining our limited perspective of reality based on finite boundaries than about recognizing and surrendering our understandings to the experiences of those who have already preceded us in death, or near-death. Observations by those with genuine near-death experiences carry more weight than the conjecture of those who only think that they know what happens after we die.

Truth is, the essence of ourselves can never truly die, because we belong to a God who created life itself. We live in a physical world with a parallel world that exists whether we can see it or not, in a place devoid of space or time, immune to any individual interpretations manufactured by human beings with limited perspectives and comprehensions.

These near-death experiences offer a glimpse into the eternal future while revealing the lasting effect of our life in the present. What we do in this world can have an everlasting effect as testified by these stories. What happens in this world can form the basis for how we live in eternity. That eternity can tell us how to better live in this world. There exists an interconnection to these two parts of our life—one being short-lived, and one lasting forever. Given this dynamic, does it not make sense to learn from those who have glimpsed some form of where you will spend eternity?

YOUR Prophetic
C O M M U N I T Y

Are you passionate about hearing God's voice, walking with Jesus, and experiencing the power of the Holy Spirit?

Destiny Image is a community of believers with a passion for equipping and encouraging you to live the prophetic, supernatural life you were created for!

We offer a fresh helping of practical articles, dynamic podcasts, and powerful videos from respected, Spirit-empowered, Christian leaders to fuel the holy fire within you.

Sign up now to get awesome content delivered to your inbox
destinyimage.com/sign-up

 **Destiny Image**

Printed in the USA
CPSIA information can be obtained
at www.ICGtesting.com
LVHW052311121023
760998LV00007B/263

9 780768 471816